125

may be kept
FOURTEEN DAYS

OTHER BOOKS BY DONALD CULROSS PEATTIE

Cargoes and Harvests (1926)
Flora of the Sand Dunes and the Calumet District of Indiana (1930)
Vence, The Story of a Provencal Town (1930)
Port of Call (1932)
Flora of the Tryon Region of North and South Carolina. *Six Parts* (1928-1932)
Sons of the Martian (1932)
The Bright Lexicon (1934)
An Almanac for Moderns (1935)
Singing in the Wilderness (1935)
Green Laurels (1936)
A Book of Hours (1937)

WITH LOUISE REDFIELD PEATTIE

Bounty of Earth (1926)
Up Country (1927)
Down Wind (1929)
The Happy Kingdom (1935)

A Prairie Grove

DONALD CULROSS PEATTIE

SIMON AND SCHUSTER · NEW YORK

1938

ALL RIGHTS RESERVED
Copyright, 1938, by Donald Culross Peattie
Published by Simon and Schuster, Inc.
386 Fourth Avenue, New York

Manufactured in the United States of America

To
PAUL SCOTT MOWRER

A PRAIRIE GROVE

I

THE ROOTS of this story, like my own, are struck deep in the black loam of the state that is shaped like an arrowhead. Where I grew up the knotted burr oaks stood, their boughs so long they arched down to the ground again. And it was under these living arches that my people came driving their wagons. They saw the green and bronze of the first of the prairie grasses, the wild gardens of the New World flora, aster and sunflower and great golden foxglove; they saw the black earth, and they called these spots the oak openings. They drove on, and the trees were spaced wider and wider, pastoral kings, each with his own realm of high meadow to shadow. They lumbered out upon the prairie, praising God for space and earth and wind. Their wagon tracks left bent the astonished grass, left flowers broken. Very slowly the most resilient culms eased up again and faced the breeze. But there were many more wagons to come, and the grass at last learned obedience.

Here was a soil with a million years of wealth in

A Prairie Grove

it, a kingdom without serious obstacle to its conquest, such space in it that men longed for a corner, women for a neighbor. Driving the plow across those seas of meadow flower, their thoughts went backward to the trees, to the gift of wood and shade. They named the faint ridges islands, and in the noon heat of their plowing they drank with thirsty eyes of those blue distant island groves.

The prairie island and its grove are like the hammock in the everglades, like an atoll in the sea, like an oasis upon the desert. It is something worth floundering and sweating for, a spot where a man can throw himself down and drink the wind and bathe in shade, where, as the blood stops pounding in his temples, he can begin to hear the birds singing deeper in the woods. The dry land and the tall trees and the short grass all make him think of home; he sees a home here before he builds it. He sees the chimney and the roof, outreached by the protective oaks, and there is something about flowers carpeting between old boles that is like the passing of a woman's skirts. So he thinks of the woman to put in the house, and of the family sounds upon the floor.

In my country, in the state shaped like an arrowhead, there are many groves. We have Elk Grove

A Prairie Grove

and Shakers' Grove, and Thatcher's Grove, and we have many ridges; there is no good country without an old highway called the Ridge Road. History moved from grove to grove along the ridges. The men rode them when the snows were deep or the rains were high, and they spared the crops thus in summer and autumn.

It requires a love of it deeply to read the slight configuration of this land. Then you may see that the old post roads of Genghis Khan were not so romantic as the Ridge Road that turns past Alison's barns, and that of the four great temperate grasslands of the world—the steppes and the veldt, the pampas and the prairies—the last are not the least.

If you cross the prairies by the train, it seems too far from here to there; that is because in the flying coach you are never anywhere. But that woman who waved at you from the porch of the white frame house under the silver poplars is in the geometric center of a circle as wide as the visible ends of the earth. She has had time, living there, to learn how mighty is distance seen horizontally. Some people only love a hill; they like their views prettily framed for them. For such, mountains are excessive, and plains give them ago-

A Prairie Grove

raphobia. But if I cannot have mountains, give me a plain where there are a hundred and eighty degrees of sky arc.

And for my peace, my habitation, and my heritage, give me an island grove upon that plain.

2

Of the prairie province they say that the seas made it. Its bones are of coral, of diatoms, and protean microscopic animals. A little later, in the course of millennia that cannot be reckoned, the fishes made it. And then, when the bed of the sea was uplifted and it became dry land, rain fell on it, and the tropical club mosses grew in the marshes tall as trees. When the Carboniferous wind blew in their awkward branches, the golden spores were piled like snowdrifts in the peat. So were the coal measures laid down, and sometimes a fern leaf, broken by an amphibian foot, fell in the ooze to leave its imprint fossil there. Students go down into mines now to look for those superscriptions of past time. A fireman, flinging coal into the engine's firebox, burns them away, in the hot prairie night, and the train tears off more miles.

The seas came back, and the continent uneasily shouldered them off again. Each time the great waters came and went they laid down the deep layers of death, out of which life was born. It took

A Prairie Grove

all of that—all that growth and dying and time measured off by the millions of years of planetary revolution around the sun—to make the Indian corn grow so tall and taste so like an August day.

In the age of man come the glaciers. They say the glaciers came and went four times. The interval of years between the third and fourth was longer than the years elapsed since the last one. In Greenland, around the polar sea, the ice is still waiting to come back. It hangs on the sides of the Rockies; even in the Berkshires there are snow holes where the ice does not melt all summer. Lower the average temperature only a little, increase the precipitation, tamper a trifle with the small but vital carbon-dioxide content of the air, and the ice might come again, sagging outward under its own weight, bulging southward, finding all ready for it—short summers, long winters.

The glaciers blocked the drainage into lakes and swamps. They made the five Great Lakes, the greatest reservoirs of pure fresh water in the world. They made old lakes now vanished, whose faint shore lines strewn with shell and gravel and clean sand are smothered now in the height of the prairie grasses.

For when a glacier leaves the field, it drops its

A Prairie Grove

scourings as it shrinks. That is where we got the boulders of Canada granite lying on the soft black velvet of our loam. My people mounted to the stirrup from such boulders, hauled to lie beneath the shady trees before the farmhouse door.

When their work was done, the glaciers had changed the life of this country. The elephant, the camel and the horse, or their ancient prototypes, were gone. So were the ferns and cycads, but the face of the land was covered swiftly, with harsh sedges in the swamps, high grasses on the upland, and a few old indomitable types of trees—the nut trees, the catkin-bearing trees, oak and hickory, cottonwood and beech and birch and elm. Add ash and linden and a low thorn forest of the stone fruits, hawthorn and crab, plum and chokecherry. The grass and the trees went to war, and they are still fighting for the land. No one knows why the forest suddenly stops, cleft away, vertical might giving place to limitless breadth. So the first explorers found it; so, the Indian said, was it always.

There are many wise guesses about the prairie. They say that grass grows best where most of the rain falls in summer. They say that if you make a map of the area having the most violent changes of temperature, it coincides precisely with the lay

A Prairie Grove

of the temperate savanna. Some think that the Indians held back the forest with fire, those fires laid to drive the game to the kill.

Of all things that live and grow upon this earth, grass is the most important. It feeds the world. Its hollow stems, its sheathing leaves and chaffy flowers, above all its unique freight of grain, describe only grass, and perhaps the sedges. These are the marsh cousins of the grasses, but they are useless, harsh, withdrawn and cryptic. Grass is generous, swift-springing, candid-growing, full of motion and sound and light. From the first oak openings of Ohio and Kentucky till it washed to the foot of the Rockies, grass ocean filled the space under the sky. Steppe meadow, buffalo country, wide wilderness, where a man could call and call but there was nothing to send back an echo.

3

Root touched root across this empire. The harsh edged leaves locked fingers, and the thoughtless west wind bore the pollen to the feathery purple stigmas of the husk-cupped flowers. In the jointed culms were water and salts, in the herbage was strength for the grazing herds, in the starch-filled seeds harvest for the mice. To the small rodents grass was forest. To the bison it was life certain underneath their hooves. Here the cock prairie chicken strutted before his wives, here in trust the lark sparrow laid her clutch of little eggs scrawled on the end with the illegible brown rune of her species, and the rattlers had a care for their frail spines when the elk walked by, terrible in branch and rut.

You may have seen Nebraska prairie, but that is low grass, bunch grass, a scattered, a semidesertic formation. You may have seen meadows, full of timothy and bluegrass, orchard grass and daisies. Those are introduced species; those are tamed Old World immigrants. The aboriginal high-grass prairie is nearly gone now. And it was something else.

A Prairie Grove

It grew taller than a certain traveler who has left us his notes, taller than this man when he sat in his saddle. It grew so thick it flung the plowshares up when they came to break it. When it burned, they say, it filled the sky with its smoke; the smoke blew through the forest belt, and when the Dakotah were rounding up the game, the Ottawa in the woods of Michigan smelt that great hunt in the air.

But we have come to subdue the grasses, to conquer the empire of locked roots. The furrows lie even and open now, in spring and fall. The geometry of fields rules the landscape. It is a land turned to use, and I do not say it is not a good use, but some purity is gone. For the fallowed field does not grow up again to prairie. Thistles and burdock come up instead; we have the tares with our wheat, and nothing wholly wild is left.

But after long hunting I have found, upon the edge of my island grove, one slim paring of forgotten virgin prairie. I knew it first because the thistles had stopped stabbing at my knees, and there was nothing here so gentle as daisies. It was not tall as the banished high grass, but it was unsullied by a single foreign weed. Between field and field of grain, it grew with a varied flourish; close

A Prairie Grove

set, coarse-stemmed, the rank flowers sprang amid the whistling grasses. Nothing grew there because it was useful; it was itself, complete, sufficient, claiming the land by the most ancient of rights.

I sat down there and looked away from the farms. I lay down and looked up at the sky. I felt this most uncorrupted earth beneath me, and all its cleanly, raw, hard strength. I knew the prairie was once all thus, and I tried to remember how that must have been. There would have been no feeling of fences around me, but only forest and grass, grass and forest, and rivers winding through. Even now was left to me that baked rosin odor of the compass plants; I saw the irritable tribal toil of the ants in their enormous mound, and in my ears the crackling of the locusts' wings and the distant anger of the crows were like primordial Amerind language.

What had happened on this natural stage? There are histories to tell me that, eyewitnesses who wrote in languages I understand. But on this turf and in the grove behind me the red men had a camp and a portage. That portage, to them but one of thousands, was, by the great accident that predestines any pattern we may see, directly in the road of history. Men of my own race had to come here. They

A Prairie Grove

were searching a passage to the China Seas, they were bringing the totem of a pale Manitou. Or they were men with lesser aims and common hungers, bringing only their right to grow where they stood and fling their seeds where they had cleared.

The bell of the church a mile north on the road rang down the fields. It is a good sound, even to unbelievers, but it broke some dream. So I stood up, the grass rising no higher than my knees. You are not so tall today, you prairie, as we are, and we shall never make you grow again, except in our thoughts.

4

THESE PAGES are those thoughts, a memory of what was gone before I came. I must remember not with my trivial faculties but with the blood that is in me. I must remember for my kind who came before me, and even for those who spoke languages that are alien to me. For they too went before me and stood where I stand, and they looked where I look, but they saw a grander and harsher world.

That world is this story, and I write it not literally but as a true legend. There are many kinds of story; we all like to hear and tell funny stories and Lincoln stories and wonder stories, and stories of the old times, lucky stories, war stories, and some of us esteem the worth of a bitter anecdote or some tale of a grand folly. We recognize that these are so many facets of the gem of truth; they give it its sparkle and its prismatic surfaces. Merely one surface is the relation called history.

The writing of history is for historians. I may not walk within their preserves. But they do not

A Prairie Grove

allow themselves to stray where I intend to go. My purpose keeps me to the theme of the island grove, the trees and the great grass, the wildfowl and the furred and antlered beasts, and tall men, very small, moving about in their roles beneath lofty boughs and across wide spaces.

We call those roles their history, and because they are finished, they seem inevitable now. But in their day these people lived as you and I do now, from moment to moment, the tense adventure of existence. Not knowing what would come, they ascribed, as you and I do, false reasons for the things they did. History sums up their story; it detects the great propulsive movements to which they were subject as are children. It cannot stop to listen to individual forgotten heart beats. But I shall listen, and I will claim the poet's right to say he knows what they think and feel who are too headlong in life to make a song of it.

The names of Father Gabriel Forreste and Father Pierre Prud'homme you will not find in all the seventy-two volumes of the *Jesuit Relations*. For one thing, they were not Jesuits. The work of the Recollet Franciscans has been neglected for the more articulate members of the Society of Jesus. I say you will not find the names of these characters of

A Prairie Grove

mine, yet they are there none the less. You will find these men in the *Relations*, unless you are blind, and you will find my Robert Du Gay in La Salle, Frontenac, Champlain. You will find the *coureurs de bois* everywhere in frontier history, and you will discover that they were the first men to reach the sources of the Mississippi, the first whites who ever gazed astounded upon the Rockies where the Big Horns jut out in the prairie province.

I guarantee, therefore, that no one in this story is wholly fictitious. It is not necessary to invent either character or detail; the gold and scarlet cloak of La Salle, the bourgeois bigotry of Father Hennepin, the humility and the death of Marquette, are matters of record. They are traditional folk airs in the great song of America.

You will not find on any map my island grove, yet it is here and I walk in it. It has had its history, predestined to it by its site between master rivers, crossed by a portage trail, and by the sort of men and women who there laid down first hearthstones, founding that honorable and half-awkward, half-lovely way of life that gave us Clemens, Altgeld, Grant, Logan, and Riley. My children are the sixth generation of their line in the grove; to go back ten generations, my people came westward by stages;

A Prairie Grove

they too are in my story, as they are in me. In old records, in county histories, in memoirs and letters I find the men and women who all over the state endured, exulted in, the privileges and pains of living in that day. I bring them to my story; I need invent little.

For the scene is all, the habitat group, man most significant in it. The drama is a biological drama; in the play we see how the white man came to the wilderness, and what happened then. The island is my stage; it would be falsifying, in effect, to name it; instead I hang out this sign: *A Wood*.

I walk beneath old trees that Du Gay might have known. I know my grove by winter and in summer; I know it through the night hours, when the vesper sparrows sing and the black-crowned herons are most active. My diaries tell me when the birds come back, when the thrush stops singing, when the first cicada praises heat. In my inventory are every one of the four hundred and fifty-three species of flowering plants that grow here. I have learned what pollinates them and what eats them and what nests among them, and what the Indians and pioneers used them for, and—have no fear—I shall not tell you much of this.

Humans have to take their place where it falls

A Prairie Grove

in the fauna. But there is no plot; this is not a novel, not a historical romance, not a popularization of history. I say that I am remembering, remembering for the trees and the great grass province and the passenger pigeons and the wild swans. I say that the coming of our species was an event, perhaps an impermanent one in the greater story. So my characters are transient, even shadowy. Individual character does not matter to Nature. In the end she absorbs all individualities; she knows only races and their rise and fall. But the ideas of our species are the human scent we leave upon the wild turf. They drift and linger on the airs after we have gone, and are the things most worth remembering about us.

5

"So we arrived," writes Father Pierre Prud'-homme, "at this little eminence lost far out upon the prairies, having covered about two hundred and forty leagues from the isle of Michilimackinac, and three hundred and sixty leagues before that from Kébec, our good Father Gabriel being in a state of prostration with his dysentery and the buffeting of the elements to which we were exposed by the ambition, restlessness, and intrepidity of the Sieur Du Gay."

FATHER PIERRE, paddling bow in the lead canoe laden with the iron forge, picks, axes, kegs of powder, brandy, and muskets, was the first of the party who saw the waving violet ribbon of smoke from the Indian village. And so he claims, as he has a way of claiming precedence all through his memoirs, that he was the first white man who ever saw this grove.

Father Gabriel Forreste had been to the Illinois country two years before; he had found the Iliniwek not here but in their winter camp. He had promised them before God to return to them and speak again

A Prairie Grove

of the Master of Life, of baptism and heaven, and he had said then that he would bring them a blacksmith to mend the guns they had bought from the Dutch beyond the mountains. But all that next summer and the winter thereafter he had lain sick and suffering in the mission at St. Ignace where the lake of the Hurons meets the lake of the Illinois. To come again, to come in the time of heat, would be death to him and he knew it. But all men have their honor, and the honor of Father Gabriel was literal. Of himself he thought that God would exact all; only toward others dared he hope that Mercy would be infinitely forgiving.

He lay on his back in the third canoe, in his gray Franciscan habit (Du Gay would have nothing to do with the Jesuits, having been to school with them and failed of attaining a vocation), and he saw the sky and the plumy reeds and the wild rice arching over him. But the leagues and the days were monotonous, monotonous with pain. God had tried his servants with the Iroquois torture fires, with fits of Huron murderous whim, with death in the rapids and slow death from hunger. Of such were the holy martyrs made. But it was the will of the Father that he, Gabriel Forreste, born only a peasant in Normandy, born to the plow and the stable dung,

A Prairie Grove

should die like this, in the ignominy of cramps and running bowels—should die, perhaps, here and now, in a shell of bark on a stream like a ditch, where the serpents basked on the bank and the swans and herons forever took screaming flight.

In his ears sputtered the curses of the two *coureurs de bois* with malediction for the *sales bêtes*, for this *sale pays*, for Du Gay, for the priests, for the canoe. "It is well," impractically wrote Father Pierre Prud'homme in after years, "to employ the *coureurs de bois* as little as possible. They think of nothing but brandy and desertion and how they may escape to the woods to lead a life of libertinage with the Indian women."

But Father Gabriel had only pity for them. Were their vile language to be cut short by an arrow or a club, they would, in their ignorant sinfulness, descend straight to hell. It was not God's will that all men should be priests, and the hungers that He had implanted in our bodies cannot always be turned to tender and moral account among heathen children. With innocent comprehension he had confessed many a wencher; for the drunkard he had only sorrow. He knew the two paddlers of this canoe, one at his head and one at his feet, for thieves whom Du Gay had tied to trees and flogged at Gros Point;

A Prairie Grove

a thought struck him, that he might die between them. And he became abashed and terrified at the audacity of a comparison that the Devil must have put in his head.

At the end of the fleet of five canoes, Robert Du Gay sat with muskets lying about his feet and in his hand the bronze plaque that was combined compass and astrolabe. Though commander, he brought up the rear because in the Detroit three canoes had dropped behind, deserted, gone back to Fort Frontenac, lost to pursuit before he knew it. Well, let them go, and might the Iroquois take them! A driving force, a fantastic hope, a gnawing vanity compelled him onward. De Soto had died a hero's death upon the great river of the south. Du Gay was not interested in the heroics of the dying; he never faced death, though he was always so near it. A man must live to get anything accomplished. But De Soto, even dead, soured his blood with envy. At Montreal he had refused a *seigneurie* larger than his native province, because he would rather carve a kingdom for himself out of the unexplored.

"We reached the summer camp of the Illinois late in the afternoon of June 10, 1673," he writes, "having been delayed by the ignorance of our Ojibwe guides who had not nearly the knowledge of the country they had led me to suppose when I paid them their wages at Michilimackinac. They took us first into a great lake surrounded by reeds over which we could not see, and covered with bustards and other wildfowl, which were so thick that they obscured one canoe from another. In this way, seeking to find egress from the lake, we wasted the quarter of a day, and were obliged to retrace our way back to the Kilimick, and take a small creek which we had missed upon ascending the stream because its mouth is so choked with flags and bushes. And so, following it for two very crooked leagues, having distant low hills covered with trees upon the east and south and nothing but prairies upon the north and west, we came at last within sight of a lofty grove, where I described the smoke from a campfire. It is necessary among even the most friendly Indians to give a warning of your approach; I therefore shouted and fired off my gun. The *coureurs* also shouted, and our Franciscan in the first canoe stood up and held aloft the peace pipe which the Ottawa chieftain had given me."

Father Pierre Prud'homme cannot be called a coward, because, though he confesses that he was terrified, he was the first to step ashore. He stood there holding up his hands. In his right hand he clutched the black crucifix; in his left he waved des-

A Prairie Grove

perately the calumet with its stem of cane and bowl adorned with eagle, crow, bluejay, and tanager feathers and trailing the long braided tresses of an Ojibwe woman, glistening with bear-fat oil.

Before the trees gave back an echo of Du Gay's musket, the entire village of the Iliniwek emptied itself, pouring out of the bark huts. The priest saw the flight of the women to the woods, dragging their children. But the braves, with bows and arrows and clubs, strode over the grass that sank gently down into sedge and water, and stopped at twenty paces from the Gray Gown. They looked to Prud'homme like children of hell. Like children they were gaudy in their tastes; a villain with a great gash on his cheek wore a chaplet of blue flowers on his head; necklaces of earthen beads brightly painted hung around thick brutal throats; their implements of death were fantastically dyed and carved. With a certain eye the priest marked down his particular enemy, the juggler with his medicine bag of raccoon skin still with the grinning face and claws upon it. And in everything they wore he saw their kinship with the world of beasts who have no souls and are the Devil's familiars. Those who went naked or as bad as naked were in themselves brute beasts, so far fallen from Adam that they never knew the

A Prairie Grove

depths of their iniquity. Father Gabriel, in his childish innocence, might say he loved these lost tribes, but Pierre Prud'homme knew the ranks of hell when he met them.

"Foreign devils," cried out the juggler in a great voice, "who are you, and what do you want with men?"

"For," writes the Sieur Du Gay, "when one speaks the word 'Illinois,' it is as if one said, in their language, 'men.' They esteem no one else to be their equals. I therefore answered them that we were Frenchmen who had come from the great captain at Kébec, and that we intended them no harm but wished to land peacefully at their settlement and exchange tokens of friendship with them."

"The Sieur Du Gay lingering in the rear," continues the narrative of Father Prud'homme, "I told them that I was sent them by the great Master of Life, and that we had brought with us Father Gabriel Forreste who had come among them two years previously at their winter camp to labor for their souls' salvation, and that now, in obedience to his oath, he was returned to them."

So the two narratives, describing always the same events, leave one to choose between them, and there is little reason to doubt that both are essentially

A Prairie Grove

truthful. Neither is complete, but they complement the great picture.

Three elder men, says the priest, advanced very slowly to meet him, the one in the middle bearing aloft a peace pipe which he held up to the sun, as if he offered it to his Maker to smoke. "Frenchmen," he said, "I take you by the hand." But he did not do so, for it was not the Illinois custom to touch hands, but only to refer to the ceremony rhetorically. "I give you tobacco," he said. But again he seemed to promise what he would presently perform. "You are welcome among us men."

The odor of bear's grease and senescent skin crept into the Father's nostrils, and as the other Indians drew casually and irregularly nearer, becoming a strengthening host, a whole racial, specific, animal taint enclosed him, intensified by the muggy sunlight of the June afternoon upon the marsh's brim. If he could scarcely support the insult to his olfactory senses now, how was he to endure a year of it?

But the Franciscan found himself deserted as Du Gay's canoe sped like a swan to the shore, and the chevalier leaped out glittering in his scarlet coat with facings of gold satin, his sword in its scabbard swinging a wide arc from his hip as he cleared the bow. He was at once surrounded by a crowd of young

A Prairie Grove

Illini who took his hat from his head and examined it. Without any intention of familiarity or insult they fingered his cloak and his beard; they weighed the scabbard in their palms. So he drew the sword forth for them and turned it this way and that in the sun to make it gleam.

But the old men, summoning four young ones, waded into the water to Forreste's canoe. When they saw him, they made the Indian sign of astonishment, which is to clap the hand over the mouth. Then the four young men lifted him out and bore his pallet on their shoulders to the shore. The *coureurs* and the Ottawas following, the whole party moved up the slope across the wild sward toward the village. Boys ran ahead and in their impatience ran back again. Men passed their hands over Father Gabriel's body, in symbol of compassion.

At the door of a house of reeds stood a very old man stark naked who held his hands up to the sun as if to shield his eyes from it. The light between his fingers fell upon a skin like bark with the brown squamae of centenarian age upon it, and made him close his mothlike lids till nothing was visible of his eyes but glitter.

The Indians halted and were silent, and Father Prud'homme held his tongue from the speech he

A Prairie Grove

had prepared, since Du Gay was silent also, and there was something in the elder which forebade interruption even of his thoughts. In the stillness, in the sunlight, a vireo spoke over its phrases like a child who does not know when the grownups are at prayer.

Then a voice, thin and light as a riffle of smoke, came from the motionless ancient. It spoke in praise of these strangers, addressing them; it lauded the sun that had grown brighter at their coming, the corn that ripened for them, the rapids that grew quiet to obey them. The poetry of ceremony rose high and cold and empty from the wrinkled lips. "I take you by the hand," he told them. "I, Nikinapi, give you tobacco. You, Father Gabriel, who speak with the Master of Life, beg him to give us years. Tell him to confuse the Iroquois. Pray him to send us buffalo. Ask him to grant us children. Our nation welcomes you, our houses are your houses. We are at peace with you. We love you."

The voice ceased. In a moment of silence the white men sought the eyes and the face for the good faith of that welcome. The face was broad and flat, and the skin did not seem to fit the cheekbones, being drum-tight; weather had thickened it so that it lacked every plane and nuance by which

A Prairie Grove

unconsciously we judge of each other's expressions. The lips were fallen into a toothless mouth, the knees bent forward, the whole body flexed at each swollen joint so that only the loin flaps hung plumb with earth. There is dignity in thin white hairs flowing to bronze shoulders, but who could tell how much of silver in the piping voice was guile? The blue Christian eyes could not read the walnut-brown ones. Who could say upon what tortures, what indecencies they had gazed in their time with pleasure?

And in that moment when the rhetoric of welcome still hung like chill upon the air, the Frenchmen felt how far they now had come, and how the wilderness had closed upon them, it might be like a trap.

6

So the first white men found it, the wooded ridge just lifted from the steppe and the swamp. A faint ridge, but one strategic, fateful, because it lay across the way men had to take, pressing westward and southward, seeking a way from the Lakes to the Gulf, seeking a portage. Here, finding its way down through the cramped and twisted drainage that the glaciers had confused, the Kilimick runs northward, toward the lakes. Further west, the Seignelay flows southward to the Father of Waters. In the spring floods, in the rarer rising of the autumn waters, a chain of sloughs connected them; a light canoe could push through the wild rice and the reed grass—so subtle is this scenery, where the faint boss of the land, less tall than a tall tree, divides the waters of the continent.

The land is drained now; the canoes are gone. Our human imprints erase natural landmarks. The eye accustomed to broken scenery finds this midland monotonous. Run by, fly by, do not stop, swift traveler; there is nothing here to interest you; you

A Prairie Grove

have said it yourself; you read no meaning; you hear no thunder in the great empty burning arch of the sky.

Only gradually the lingerer grows conscious of fine shadings, of great meanings in slight symbols. At last he can hear the great voice that speaks softly; he can see the swell and fall upon the flank of a statue carved out in a whole continent's marble.

The Illinois came here, not foreknowing this grove's destined role, but placing their summer camp strategically, on the crossroads of the forest game and the prairie game. The human animal, the red man, was a carnivore, who hunted, like the wolves in packs, the other beasts about him. An obligate nomad, he went where the game went, and on foot he chased his food, his clothing and his implements that arrogantly fled before him. He followed the game southward, harrying, in winter, marching in the trail of its dung, streaking after it like the cowbirds that flew to sit upon the rumps of the buffalo and devour the ticks and flies.

With an elk tine the women dug a seed hole for the maize. In a raccoon skin the jugglers carried medicine, and when the wild swans went over, a storm of arrows shot from arches bent to breaking struck across their flyway and brought them plum-

A Prairie Grove

meting to earth. Then the girls must set them away in brine against the winter famine. Swan feathers blew about the camp then, and with owl's feathers and heron's plumes and metallic glitter of teal and mallard and goldeneye, they went to make the magic of the medicine lodge; they winged the arrows, trailed in splendor from the calumet, or were thrust in the greased black hair.

Here was a species whose talons were arrows, whose speed was in their cunning, whose strength was the prairie fires they lighted that ran without need of breath or water, and so outran the stumbling herd of heaving flanks and lolling tongues. They ate as the beasts ate, ravenous and gorging in hours of abundance; they all knew famine in its season, and like carnivores they had to eat then the memory of old feasts. They took some thought against the morrow, but never enough. Yet in the midst of abundance, they were not wasteful; they were too ignorant to kill for sport. The animals too, they thought, had souls; they must not be insulted or their spirits broken; the herbs were in the earth's keeping, and when they gathered their simples they asked her pardon. "I take these thy hairs, Nokomis, grandmother, and I thank you and ask your pardon."

A Prairie Grove

One must not think that they were sentimental; they took what they needed because they saw that all things take what they need. Why not, in a world so rich?

And in all historic time there has never been abundance like it. Not in the temperate world, where men are restless, where the speeding years flash past the gay dress and the nakedness of the seasons. It was a very long time ago that Greece lost her forests and that the circular hunt of the Tartars swept the great game from the Asian steppes. But in our own yesterdays the elk still lifted confident antlered heads unafraid of a bullet; the mast of the forest fed ten million pigeons; trees fell only from rot or wind. Ducks still built their nests neighbor to men, that now must hide them away in a last borderland of reeds. There was an amply filled solitude, a yet undestroyed balance in all the land then. It was a balance kept by harsh laws past our reconstructing. Yet all things enjoyed then the right to live, and to death they were submissive without thought. Amidst such prodigality there was little need to plant, and the buffalo calved in the deep grass without tending.

We have substituted another life, one that without our mastery upon it runs back to weak forms,

A Prairie Grove

dry udders, thorns without fruit, and the smutted kernel. It is our way, and it is a great way, with a sweet traditional taste to it, and I love the barnyard with its fowl out of Asia, the haymow with its fermenting grasses brought here from the cultural sources of our civilization. I like the starlings and the sheep and the horses mighty and diffident; I like the white little hams of the children squatting down to entice the geese with grain. These are our belongings; this is our flesh; this way must we go.

But lift your hand from the land, or let the outraged earth turn on you—and the wild comes back, an embittered wild. There was never a tempest that so darkened heaven as the great dust storms blown from lands tortured into too much bearing. Strip the ancient herbs away, the lance-tall grasses with their pennant chaff, and in revenge the thistles spring— rabble running where the old kings stood. There will be crows here to pick the last grain we sow. But never again the pigeons, the bison, the man holding his fingers to the sun.

7

Pierre Prud'homme has set it down as his opinion that the aboriginal Americans are the lost tribes of Israel. How else indeed account for a people not otherwise mentioned in the history of creation?

The Recollet was not a very satisfactory ethnographer. He recorded what he learned of the Indians as one implicitly disapproving. He pointed out their customs largely as an indication of how much would have to be altered. But even he did not expect to change their Oriental features—the broad flat faces, the shovel-shaped teeth, the wide and heavy noses with rounded nasal gutters such as we see among us only in children. He was observant enough to notice the shortness of the Indian head, the lack of frontal development which is replaced by bosses on the sides of the skull. Bumps of perversity, they must have seemed to the zealot.

These poor children of the prairies, as Prud'homme called them, did not possess the wheel. Cut off thus from easy land transport, they were made

A Prairie Grove

dependent upon the rivers and the lakes. Lacking the horse, they had to pursue their game on foot. In these wants they were, of course, no worse off than the rest of their Algonkian relatives. With these relatives they might be at war, but they did recognize a language affinity; if a man could speak the Illini tongue he could make shift to understand the Miamis, the Potawatomis, the Mascoutens, and the Ojibwes. From Kébec to Maine, and west to the Mississippi, the Algonkians held sway, but for the indomitable salient of the Iroquois. They were the birchbark-canoe Indians, the traditional scalpers of Colonial atrocity tales. They were, also, the Indians whom the Dutch and English robbed and cheated, the Indians to whom they gave raw whiskey and gonorrhea. Their tragedy does not make them all noble red men. Before you sentimentalize them you have to accept the fact that they lived on terms of amity with hordes of lice, that they lustily enjoyed torturing their enemies, that they were as keenly addicted to various perversions as ever the civilized, and that their boasted democracy did not for a moment contemplate raising the Amerind woman above the status of an animal of burden. In fact, other beasts lacking for this end, she was that animal.

A Prairie Grove

The Illinois were among the most affable of all the Algonkians. They were also among the most treacherous, perverse, and cowardly. Their treachery, indeed, brought on their easy extermination by a brother tribe. Other Indians had no use for them. Only a saint could have loved them. It was on this point that Father Prud'homme differed so widely from his coreligionist.

To the practical priest it seemed that the Illini were no further advanced upon salvation and civilization than Adam, naked outside the garden. He thought them miserably housed in their rectangular buildings of bark supported on poles; here several families would live together, half a dozen men with all their wives and children sleeping about on mere shelves. The women wove a little, in the fiber of barks, using the fingers only and working from the top of the loom downward. Of rushes and splint they could contrive a little basketry, though never of so advanced a type as the coiled sort. Their pottery was of a primitive order. When they passed you a dish it was a boat-shaped piece of bark.

The clothing troubled the good father like an unregretted sin. Children and young braves went naked by preference. When they arrayed themselves it was in the skins of beasts, so a sleeved coat, a breech clout and leggings of leather and moccasins with drooping flaps passed for finery. Women wore skirts and jackets of hide. Yet simple as their wants were, these savages already had avarice for the rare and costly. Pipestone from the headwaters of the Mississippi, copper from Lake Superior, grizzly-bear claws from the Rockies were wares of price.

But the pen of a narrator even so hostile as Prud'homme could not pass over the skill of this human animal upon the water. Where the Sioux spin round and round in bowls of hide, as Herodotus tells that the Mesopotamians used to do, the Algonkian, in his canoe, skimmed like a swan over still waters; he shot rapids like a salmon, steered by a tremor of the wrists. From the boats, deer were killed, and sturgeon shot. The deer and the elk and the buffalo were a lifelong study to the Illinois. They were sensitive to a trace, a smell, a sound of their quarry. They knew, indeed—in their aboriginal darkness so deplored by the priest—all that they needed to know to exist in the North American fauna, as hawks know their business, or rattlers how to survive.

So far the condescending pen of my leading authority has restrained itself. But when Father Prud'homme comes to the medicine lodge, his anger and horror cannot be checked. In its iniquity it surpasses

A Prairie Grove

for him even the libertine character of the people and the immodesty of their dress.

I find indeed that in the speed which outrage gave his pen he has confused the *gens* or family-group fetishes with the midewiwin or medicine lodge. The fetishes, his hosts did not disguise from him, were bundles of human scalps, amulets made of a buffalo's tail or the claws of a grizzly bear or the mummified remains of almost anything from which at last, perhaps, the stench had departed, but not the manitou. Each group—the fish *gens*, the bear *gens*, the frog, river-monster, and thunderbird *gentes*, each had its clan bundle, and Father Prud'homme records that he has seen a man beat the bundle when there was ill luck, fondle and adore it when fortune smiled.

To be an Algonkian in the days of heathen innocence was to walk the world with spirits. In all things there was manitou, boding ill or good for humans. The origin of your clan bundle was lost in myth and dream. You lived by a world of dreams, and what you dreamed would happen it was your duty to make come to pass. To dream of many elk was a sign of life; to dream of bears was death. In pain you must not cry out. What you loved best you must be most ready to give away, but over your

A Prairie Grove

moods society expected you to exercise small control. A man in an ill humor was considered irresponsible as if insane. They gave him his way; they made him presents; until, his good cheer restored, his impulses grew less dangerous. A man was a warrior and a hunter, but never for a moment menial. A woman was a slave and just possibly a pet; she was the earth you planted. Between these extremes Algonkian society found no regular recognized adjustment for anyone who wished to be less sheerly male or female. Yet there would crop up women with a capacity for leadership, men with no taste for war and with the desire to make something beautiful. The boy who wanted to weave a pattern, to make a design of his own dreaming, had to put on skirts and dwell among maids. The woman leader must endure male hardship and stifle instincts.

This was the pattern, this the ideal. In fact, however, individuals did not attain to it always. All braves were not brave, and Indians could melt or run away like children. Many squaws berated and tyrannized over men, less obedient than the fertile earth. People went berserk sometimes; Indians recognized criminals among them. Sex would not stay in molds; tenderness and romance, though quite

A Prairie Grove

unprovided for by the conventions, broke through upon occasion.

You lived your life to the dance. You danced to bring the buffalo, you danced to lure the elk. You danced up the rain, you danced sex and sorrow, ghosts and dreams, sickness and medicine, violent death and torture. Dance was not social, not a spectacle in the sense that paid and trained performers make a ballet for inert, incapable spectators; dance was above all not, usually, sexual—not a pantomime of courtship like the minuet, an approved embrace, like our modern dancing. It was religious; it was literally a life and death matter. It was self-expression, a democratic art; it was one of life's great rhythms, like breathing and the beating of the heart. And with dance went the pulse throb of the drums, and singing. Captives led to the stake sang a death song—a ceremonial song learned long in advance and apparently in preparation for just such a contingency. They would have omitted it as little as we omit the march from a wedding procession. Without song and dance life had no more dignity than the ways of brute beasts.

So the red man lived, clothed in his paints, an animal in the North American fauna who recognized with more candor than we his fellowship with the

A Prairie Grove

beasts. He had found his place in that fauna; he wasted not, neither did he defile. When he had eaten a beaver, he did not throw the bones to the dogs, lest other beavers should be insulted. Before he set out to kill the buffalo, he sat down a while and cried tears for them. He worshiped the North and the South, the East and the West. The tobacco field was a holy place; one should not jest in it, or even speak of common things there.

And he is gone now, for his descendants have Ford cars and go to the motion pictures. They are ashamed and ape the white man and strive to compete with him in his world. No one who has seen reservation Indians has seen much more than beggars. The bodily type, the spiritual force, the brute beauty have been destroyed by dependence, confinement, disease, and miscegenation. But once they were here, the great people, and they slapped this ground with their dancing feet in exultation.

8

THE MAN who began to wake up slowly out of a dream was not the Recollet Franciscan, not the alien in the camp of savages, but only the child Jacques he had been born, Jacques Forreste. He was a child conscious of somehow needing his mother. Very slowly his identity, his situation, returned to him. He felt the earth under his back, an ant upon his hand, the soreness in his bowels as he stirred a little, and he knew that his three hours of night serenity were over.

He remembered now how he had forced himself to remain till midnight present at the great council and ceremony of reception. He had sat through the feasting upon wild goose and sagamité, young bear and prairie chicken and chicks in the egg. Ceremonial dogs had been offered; the chief apologized that they had had to be killed swiftly instead of allowing them to die properly by hanging them to poles by their hind legs. It had been a dangerous breach of etiquette to refuse this fare, but Du Gay and Prud'homme had explained that in France such was

A Prairie Grove

not the custom. And Indians understand that custom is immutable.

Then they had brought him here, out under the burr oaks, and a woman and a boy had massaged his limbs with wildcat grease till the aching fatigue melted from him. He saw the woman at last rise with a grimace of pain in her cramped limbs and tired muscles, and the boy in the moonlight showed a face drained of color. The priest knew that he was eased by communicating his weariness to others, and he was humble in his heart at the goodness that God had planted in children so far removed from His Kingdom and His Word. As he dropped to sleep he was conscious of the steady, rhythmical screaming of a baby far away on the other side of the village. He knew the child was sick, but he could not keep his eyelids apart, though he tried to pray for it before he slept.

Now God's day was coming, the beautiful light He had made. It was not surprising that the Indians should worship the sun; it was a premonition in them of the true faith. Lying on his back and looking upward, he saw the sunlight bathing the lofty heads of the trees. There was a first shaken rapture of a bird, a voice of gladness that another night had passed without death by violence. He

A Prairie Grove

could see, high on a bough, the singer facing the sunrise that just flushed its breast, and he had noticed that at dawn and sunset birds always turn like this, as the old men turned their faces and held up their hands to the light.

Now the light moved down the boles of the trees. Then it was on the grass, giving back color to the flowers. Now he could feel it on his hand, that lay weak and idle and ashamed of being so. Presently it slipped to his face and fingered it, and he closed his eyes and gave himself up to it, and to all the birds now singing—simply, without thinking or praying. From the marsh water came the croaking and harsh screaming of many waterfowl, where someone had disturbed them. He opened his eyes, and idly watched the toil of a spider on a dew-hung web. How could this little beast know such art and craft? he wondered. How, unless God had always been here, even in this wilderness?

He roused himself and got to his knees and, bent with cramps, he said his Pater Noster and Hail, Mary!

The waterfowl had risen with imprecations to heaven at the step upon the shore of the Sieur Du Gay. He was the sort of man who could not sleep. He could not go off guard; though he would un-

A Prairie Grove

buckle his sword and lay it down beside him, his hand slept on it naturally. Indians might snore away their time in torpor; the *coureurs de bois*, like the common rascals and sluggards they were, roused late after late carousing. For himself, he drank without pleasure; wine was a confusion to the clear intoxicant of his ambition. He did without woman, unwilling to share himself with less than his plans. He slept a little, grudgingly, out of animal necessity, as one gives time to eating and bathing. In their day, all things would come to him—banqueting and soft bedding, too. He wanted a wife, not women, and not so much a wife as a queen. He saw her royally, as someone to wear the jewels of fabled Cibola. His intention for her was dynastic, to give him sons to hold up his hand, so that what he wrought might stand in his name.

He liked beginnings; he liked dawn, when dullards were abed and knaves not yet at their trade. He liked the empty room of day, the scene unpossessed. He had no idea, as we have, that to be a beginner was the whole of his fate.

That intense preoccupation of his was not born of commercial genius; he saw the beauty of his kingdom. On his way down to the river, striding through the long shafts of sunlight, he beheld the dew.

A Prairie Grove

And he paused to see a grass stem bent down with it, the gathering of drop to drop until the whole round opal, flashing blue and ruby, sped down the channel of the blade to earth, and the grass, having dropped its tribute into the ground, relaxed upward in the freshened air.

All his kingdom over, it was thus each morning, a diamonded splendor from pure naked sky to the very roots of the grass. Here in the tree boles was timber for ships and forts, for gunstocks, ax handles, and at last for homes. His ideas were not genuinely military, like those of his lieutenant Pons whose arrival from Canada he awaited. He planned forts, but only to protect the fur trade. And there were furs in this country to make beggars of the big-nosed merchants of Novgorod!

The *coureurs de bois,* whatever the priests might think of them, he saw as links in the great chain that must carry marten and beaver and ermine to France. He could use the greed in them; they had what Indians never had, the true instinct to exploit, the curiosity to go and find. They had in the end more sheer endurance, being single-minded; they never turned back because a dream warned them that they should, or because a woman in her *règles* had touched them. What they asked was to

A Prairie Grove

live beyond the realm of law. They demanded the illusion of working for themselves; they wanted to enjoy the vices of freedom. He, Du Gay, was willing to let them have these, and if he foresaw a hybrid race he knew there was no danger in it. Such children would not have in them the clan strength of either blood; they could be molded to a new pattern.

He reached the river's marge, and found the wildfowl zoned according to their dispositions. From the shore the herons stormed up heavily, night shadows cupped under the camber of their wings, reluctance for the earth in the trailing wake of their legs. Blackbirds scolded and spattered out of the green shaken reed world, and next, beyond the floating lilies, the ducks struggled and ran upon the water and flickered off long and low, drops flashing from the oily feathers. There were left the killdeer, half afraid to go, crying out as they circled and settled again, as if he had wounded them, had wounded them, had wounded them! At the last minute a king rail ran past his feet with a piercing cry from the full rose-brown breast; out of the cattails came the soft thudding, as if on wood, of the hen rail calling her chicks. Du Gay caught just a glimpse of them as they toddled, fat, fluffy, and sable-black, across the mud, peeping out of slate-blue bills; then they gained the water and sailed diminutively into haven.

Du Gay had for them a smile in his beard. He had no need of their lives, no wish for less than the vast animal fertility of this country. He saw it as never anything but young, a colony of raw materials, a source and storehouse.

Robert Du Gay knew where he stood in this world. In Old France he belonged to the *petite noblesse*. He could have stayed at home and enjoyed the right to carry a sword, to order the drums to be beaten, to keep doves in the turret of his little château in Picardy, to marry a cousin with a little money and a little pelvis, and, if he had the clothes for it, he could go to court and intrigue to be noticed. In New France he was under the Governor at Kébec; he had a commission and a charter that might be revoked or superseded at any moment; he had enemies in both countries, men who had tried to prevent everything he wanted to do. Yet none of them had a constructive idea. Not one of them was willing to go where he, Du Gay, went; they only bribed Indians to set his ship afire; they thought of duties to clap upon his peltry. Maggots!

His loyalty to his monarch was intense. Louis XIV was a king who knew how to make a throne

A Prairie Grove

glitter. Like the Indians, he took the sun for his symbol. He could use the priests without being used by them; he played off England and Spain, and turned the weakness of Germany to account. Du Gay admired Louis' minister Colbert; there was a man who knew what money was for! But for the rest of the aping crowd he had no use, no envy. While the diplomats were squabbling whether Spain or France should have a little county like Roussillon, Spain was entrenching herself in the New World; her hand was upon California, her claims went indefinitely northward and eastward. The mouth of the Mississippi was already Spain's, if De Soto's claim could not soon be invalidated by the tangible fact of a powerful French colony. In matters of the sword Spain was a steel realist; by the instrument of the mission she would make of the Indians a pacified subservient village people.

Along the Atlantic coast the Dutch and English stretched an unbreakable cordon. Toward the Indian they had a policy of steady removal or extermination; they were set against mingling the blood of the races. They sent their rum ahead of them, corroding the barriers that should withhold them. New France, between Spain and England, was still only a name, a hope, a fresh wind running ahead, lifting a flag in the forest.

9

"There is no use in trying to shorten Indian ceremonials," writes Du Gay. "It is a sign of enmity not to allow one's self to be honored to the fullest extent within the power of the tribe. We therefore submitted ourselves, Father Prud'homme and I, to the celebrations which our hosts devised for us, Father Forreste being ill and attended by Indian women, while to our *coureurs* I judged it wise to give liberty to hunt and otherwise disport themselves."

THE MORNING was already warm when the two Frenchmen were conducted with honor through the grove to the place of ceremony. The braves were painted black and yellow and red, out of respect for the rank and dignity of their guests. Some wore their hair hanging down upon the left side, the right shaved or burned away; some carried the lock upon the right; all brought their weapons and strode along with their ceremonial skin cloaks swinging beast tails behind them. To the Frenchmen it seemed that they walked, two humans, in a troop of skins and feathers, tails and claws. Yet here were men

A Prairie Grove

to be dealt with; here were human intelligence and guile and pride of race; these beings had martial traditions of bodily courage and they recognized objects of veneration. It was well to keep all this in mind just when they seemed most childish, most generous, or most bestial.

Women in their skin dresses stood silent but curious all along the way. Children and tall boys ran beside the defile, naked but for some shell ornament at the throat or in the ear. In the conventional silence of the occasion only the voice of an enormous young man, some master of arms for these rites, was heard continually calling out that a way must be made, a way must be made! These people were in their summer capital. Over three hundred rectangular bark lodges formed their village; the smoke of their fires went up in proud spirals or was caught by a wind promising rain and sent swirling about the glistening legs of the processionaries. It brought the odor of meat, of an immense preparatory festal roasting. The cuts would be charred, the Frenchmen knew, almost to coals; there was no telling what unthinkable entrails, what unholy beasts would be offered them.

The scene of the dance was set in the shade of hickory and ash. Bright-dyed mats had already been

A Prairie Grove

tramped into place upon the springy sward, and upon arrival the braves all threw down their weapons in a heap and immediately squatted or lay down upon the grass. The Recollet and the captain sat in the fashion of white men, on their buttocks with their knees drawn up. Then the chief, Nikanapi, began to speak, explaining that they would present their guests with the calumet, to be used as an emblem of peace and safety when they went among the evil tribes of the south.

The first figure of the ceremony was not impressive to the Europeans. A dancer pranced heavily but not without cadence upon the mats, offering the calumet to the four quarters of the earth and to the sun; then he passed it to every lip to smoke. For the second figure a drum was used, and a little rattle shaken so that it kept up an insect singing, and two dancers very slowly pantomimed a combat, one having only the calumet with which to defend himself. Then Nikanapi arose and, taking the calumet, began, as it seemed to his foreign hearers, to boast childishly of his exploits. When he had done, he presented it to Du Gay.

It was high noon before they returned to the village for the feasting. Silence was still observed, but this time, Prud'homme suspected, out of pre-

A Prairie Grove

occupation with the stomach. The first course was a great wooden platter of sagamité, corn boiled in water and seasoned with fat; the chief filled a spoon with it and placed it in Du Gay's mouth. He repeated this three times, and then fed the priest in the same fashion. Fish were brought, and Nikanapi removed the bones with his own fingers, blew on the flesh to cool it, and then tenderly popped the morsels by finger between the lips of his guests. The ceremonial dogs were then brought on, as a matter of tradition, and sent silently away, out of respect for the alien and contrary custom of the Frenchmen. For the last course the buffalo was dragged to the center of the circle; the chief arose and cut out the hot and nearly liquid fat with a knife; this he fed to those whom he honored, as if they had been small birds.

With a rising gorge Du Gay got to his feet and thanked his hosts for their goodness. He said that he would speak to them by four presents, and laying at the feet of the chief a mirror, he told them that he was journeying peacefully to visit the nations whose hunting ground lay beyond theirs. By the second present, a string of glass beads, he announced that the great Master of Life who had made them had so far taken pity upon them as to instruct them

A Prairie Grove

by this Gray Gown in His will. By a cloak of Flemish velvet he informed them that the great Captain of the French at Kébec wished them to assist him to build a fort here, in order to hold the ground against their enemies the Iroquois and the English. Last, he gave a musket, and by this present desired of them to obtain all the information possible about the rivers and the nations of the lands where the birds went in winter.

Nikanapi's reply would have done honor to a Spanish ambassador, Du Gay thought. He promised everything without allowing the hearer to infer that diplomatic courtesies could be literally interpreted. He begged his guests not to risk themselves to the cruel nations of the south, not to encounter the evil monsters who lived in the rivers, not to carry guns and powder to the Osages. "But remain here," he said, "O Frenchmen! Take pity upon us, teach us, who are only children before you!" Then he sat down, and the wrinkled eagle film fell equivocally over his eyes.

That afternoon the braves gave a match of lacrosse in honor of the visitors. There was a bear dance, where the performers wore immense and comic phalli; that night another feasting fol-

A Prairie Grove

lowed, so prolonged that the sated revelers rose now and again to go aside and put their fingers down their throats till they vomited and could eat again. Du Gay and Prud'homme availed themselves of the custom by which you might beg a neighbor to eat for you. That night the women were allowed to dance; it was, fortunately for the good Father, very decorous and uninteresting dancing, done far from the firelight, in the shadows of the trees looking at the stars.

Beyond the circle of the campfire lights, beyond the bobbing women dancers, beyond those trees painted too with light were other trees standing in a cool and mighty darkness. There the sward was fresh and untrodden, the bough unbent, the earth undefiled. There the odors were those of leaf rot, of fungus, dampness, fern and flowering things; beast smells there were too, but faint, discreet, the modest trace of those who keep themselves hidden. Yes, there was the great decency of the unhuman, out there in the forest, of animals who have no need of shame, being no more than animals.

The ducks rafted in coveys on the river and drowsed with their bills nestled into their backs. The coots there swung around slowly in the water

A Prairie Grove

on one green foliate foot. The herons humped morosely in the trees, plumes elegant and sulky between shoulders. The chick rails would be under soft pinions now. Down the aisles of the wood the fireflies put out their little green lights.

10

Father Prud'homme in his account of the Illinois admits that they are a very affable people. They seldom say no to any proposition; they offer to give you anything, but like Spaniards they do not suppose you are so barbarous as to take them at their word. He had seen service in the cause of God among the Iroquois, and their hatred of the true faith and of the French was fierce and open. With the Illinois, Father Pierre never knew where he stood. When he asked them to be silent and listen to him, they were silent; he could say, "Stop smoking." "Kneel down." "Bow your head." And the rules governing the conduct of Illinois life required his hosts to do whatever he suggested.

He gave them little cards and pictures of the Ascension of the Virgin, the sorrowing of Mary, the descent from the Cross, the parting of the wicked from the saved upon Judgment Day, and of the Nativity. In these the Indians showed intense interest and delight; they regarded them as fetishes of the clan bundle of the Franciscan phratry, and they wore

A Prairie Grove

them around their necks with their wampum. Crucifixes and rosaries went the same way. The origin myths of these strange fetishes absorbed and perplexed the good Father's listeners. Crucifixion was a bad thing, they thought, but the Iroquois were worse than the Jews.

Once Father Prud'homme found where a child had forgotten the colored card given him, among the grass. The wind that is made by the flapping of one wing of the great bird chained in the west had blown it thoughtlessly into a little puddle full of sky. He took it up and wiped it gently with the heel of his palm; it represented the child Mary standing at the knee of Saint Anne, and both were smudged and rain-soaked. He tried to find forgiveness in his heart; these naked little ones with their yellow bodies, their unreadable and, it seemed to him, hardened faces, their wolfish teeth and lank hair, were not in their hearts wicked. You could not compare them, for instance, to heretics in Europe, to Protestants who rejected salvation wilfully. The Indian children must be, he knew, his hope; but he realized that as yet they only learned to pray for the reward of a red bead for a boy, a needle for a girl.

Already knowing Ottawa, Father Prud'homme

A Prairie Grove

could make the adults understand him, and he tried to compile a dictionary of Illinois words in order that he might preach in their own language to the slower-witted. Young men and even sometimes women amused themselves boundlessly by giving him names for things that made him blush, and when he refused to write these down they were swept by gales of laughter. The Illinois, indeed, were endlessly fond of jokes; they were solemn only in council. Men, in the idleness that occupied most of their days, chatted and gossiped like old crones; the women, like beasts of burden, had less to say. Girls were gay only before marriage.

The Illinois tongue was extensive enough, but sadly impoverished in equivalents for the vocabulary of the great Hebrew stylists. When the priest recited the Twenty-third Psalm, he knew that to Indian ears he was saying:

"The great Spirit rounds up the buffalo for me. Now I will never need to go without anything. He takes me along beside the stinking waters; he makes me lie down on the green prairie. He greases my hair with running grease; my bark bowl slops over."

But Father Prud'homme was not by any means proposing, even if it could be done, to put a vernacular Bible in the hands of the ignorant. The train-

A Prairie Grove

ing of his order taught him rather to reveal portions of the truth, as the simplest of God's children were able to ingest it.

But in one respect he was like most missionaries; he was profoundly troubled by the indecency of nudity; he did not see how a people could be kept from constant preoccupation with lewd thoughts while they lived amidst scenes that could only make him think of a bawdyhouse. He did not allow boys and girls to attend his class at the same time, and presently, he records, he had the extreme happiness of making the little girls shy, so that when he entered the bark hut where he was to teach them they gathered shreds of deerskin to them with what he hoped was modesty. You could do nothing with the boys who were so proud of the tattooing on their backs and stomachs that they would by no means cover themselves.

The wives dressed modestly enough, but he could arouse no spirit in them against polygamy. A man would marry a girl and adopt all her sisters as second wives and concubines; they could not understand that this was incestuous. The younger sisters were glad that the chief wife was not a harsh, jealous stranger; the man was content that his women, being of one family, did not quarrel. Behold the prairie chicken,

A Prairie Grove

who has many wives. See how the bull buffaloes rule their cows. The elk drives his herd of womenfolk before him; the does among themselves are loving; their master keeps the wolves away; their fawns, acknowledging one father, are all brothers and sisters. If the great Master of Life did not wish it thus, he would change it.

"How would you have it?" Father Forreste answered when his brother brought him his troubles. "These people are between the Iroquois and the Sioux. Their men die young; they are harried and killed and captured. And when a man meets his death, his brother, as with us, must assume the care of the dead man's family. The widow thinks in her simplicity that she is honored and loved when she too is taken to the man's mat. These women and children would suffer and starve but for this savage way of life. It is not ours to reproach them; we must rather spread peace among these children of the woods and prairies. They have only one besetting sin and weakness that is the cause of all their other transgressions. They do not know the brotherhood of man; they hate and kill. They have not found the love of God, to make them good and comfort them. When they have given up the warpath, then there will be as many men as women. Young maidens will

A Prairie Grove

be sought after and so they will no longer be so easy. God in His time will teach them."

In spite of all he could do, well and zealous though he was, Father Prud'homme could never obtain the influence over the savages that his confrere had. The sickness of the old priest did not make him an object of contempt; the Indians admired the stoicism with which he bore himself. They discussed among themselves the course of his malady with a solicitude in detail that would have shocked the decency of Prud'homme. They understood that he did indeed speak with the Great Spirit. He lived apart, fasting and suffering and waiting, as they supposed, for a dream. In that dream his manitou would tell him what to do, and it would be something difficult and probably, indeed, fatal. But whatever it was, it would be done for the good of all his clan, and for the good of the Indians. They knew real love when they met it; they recognized the strength of devotion when it touched them. And when from its traveling case he drew forth the chalice set with jewels and washed with gold, and a sunbeam piercing through the oak leaves dazzled on its rim, they covered their eyes with their hands to show him that they saw and were amazed.

I I

THE DISSENSIONS between Du Gay and Father Prud'homme had begun when they came out from France together. There had been a flock of girls on board who were on their way to Canada to find husbands and make wives for soldiers and trappers. They were girls without dowries, orphans, children left on the steps of convents, young women without hope of happy settlement in France. On the sunlit deck they sewed and danced and chattered; they complained of the salt stiffening their hair but they laughed when the spray dashed through its own rainbow across the gunwales and flecked their lips and fell into their laps. These girls had led cramped lives; they were going out into a world without restraint, and they knew it. The purpose of their journey was uppermost in their heads, and they began to taste their freedom by flirting with the sailors.

In his berth on a moonlit night Father Prud'homme could hear their feet directly over his head. While he was trying to read his breviary the rhythmi-

A Prairie Grove

cal tramp and click of the dancing interrupted his thoughts. If he knew men, and as a confessor he thought he did, the sailors could not well be thinking of anything except flying skirts. When midnight struck he came on deck and ordered the girls to their beds. There was no meekness in their replies; their hearts were already full of license, and to make matters worse, the Sieur Du Gay stepped out of the shadow of the mast and in their presence took their part.

"You are an old pedant," said Du Gay.

"God at any rate did not fail to give me a vocation," retorted Father Prud'homme. But, as he records, he did not then know that Du Gay had left the Jesuit college; later he apologized for the thoughtless insult of his reply.

And matters went on thus, the two of them well fitted to annoy each other. That the Governor of New France had sent them out from Kébec together, each took as a cross to be borne.

The policy of Du Gay was to prepare the Illinois for resistance against the Iroquois. He wanted to arm them, to train them for a stationary life of resistance. If the Dutch were going to sell them brandy—and nothing, it seemed, could prevent it—then it

A Prairie Grove

was economically and strategically sounder that the savages should get French brandy through Kébec.

Principles like these were thorns in the side of the Recollet. Du Gay was opposed to a formal marriage between the *coureur de bois* and the Indian woman; his men must have no attachments of family or property to any one spot. Like himself they must be free to take all risks, and if the lure of fresh pleasures among women would help to draw them beyond the horizon, so let it be.

The activities of Father Pierre seemed to put in jeopardy the relations so perilously balanced over the chasm of treachery. How perilous they were Du Gay alone envisaged. Every guest in an Indian camp is an expense. It was not money that he cost the Indians, but food. Wilderness hospitality has always demanded lavishness; it cannot be refused, lest the host himself some day want among strangers. In a prolonged stay the traveler creates dearths which cannot really be paid for, and Du Gay was, all unknown to the Illinois, lingering for the arrival of Captain Pons with thirty men. Without their help he could not man the chain of forts that must rise in the wilderness to hold it. When they came there would be thirty more mouths to feed, more ceremonial

A Prairie Grove

feasts for the whole village, more love affairs with their perpetual danger from the Indian humors.

The zeal of Father Prud'homme had not waited a week to manifest its indiscretion. He had been seen before daylight listening and peering around the medicine lodge. There was no doubt, of course, that the juggler was a grasping, mean, and ridiculous trickster, but Du Gay knew better than to let it be known that he thought so. Father Prud'homme, however, had attended a dance given by the mother of a sick baby, had objected to what he called the indecency of the performance, and finally had publicly unmasked one of the medicine man's simplest conjuries. When the juggler sucked a stone out of the child's breast, the priest had reached into his enemy's robes and removed a handful of stones, a toad, and a very small rattler with its fangs drawn. The next day, when he opened the case of his little traveling chapel in the presence of the curious crowd that always gathered to see him perform a mass, a toad jumped out of the monstrance.

The child was dying, and Du Gay knew it. So did Father Prud'homme when the woman at last brought the little naked thing like a picked crow for baptism. He gave the little soul to God, understanding quite clearly that upon its mother's part baptism was per-

A Prairie Grove

formed in the hope that the foreign medicine would save the child's life. Two days later it died in convulsions, and the medicine man came to the mother's hut and told her why.

When he had gone, the Gray Gown entered and asked her to rejoice that her child was saved from burning and was nestling on the bosom of Mary, the Woman-who-went-to-the-sky.

The baby was wrapped in rabbit skins and put at the door of the lodge, doubled up like a child in the womb, and on the second day the little face was painted and he was lowered into a grave with a kettleful of sagamité, a rattle, and belts and necklaces of wampum. There were no tears except the mother's. In a year from this day, the relatives explained to the Frenchmen, there would be a dance of mourning, a funeral feast, and then everyone would weep.

From that time on, the influence of Prud'homme over the women and children was weakened. The most damaging effect of the incident was the quarrel that it precipitated between Du Gay and the priest. The angry words were not understood by the Indians, but they were overheard, and the rift injured the prestige of the foreign power. Every week that the white men remained among the Indians, the less they could appear like divinities. When they were

A Prairie Grove

cut they bled; when they were hungry they were irritable; when they labored they grew weary. The *coureurs'* women know their mortal weakness—found them, indeed, far easier to persuade and wheedle than their own males. These guests had powder, liquor, guns, and wampum that were destined to be given to Osages and Ioways; temptation glinted opaquely in the eyes of their hosts. Yet every night the white men had to sleep. They had to lie down, sword and crucifix put aside, and trust themselves to the mercies of the night and those that walk in the night.

12

I know that night. I know the fireflies' hour that comes when the dog-day cicadas cease the shrill shearing of their songs. Sometimes the thrush has last benedictions to say. The burning fields have still some heat to breathe out, and it is not night yet when I can feel that air upon my cheeks, hot as the blood in them. It is night when the ponds throw up dampness, an odor rank and stagnant. It is night when the woods surrender hoarded coolness, with the smell of high weeds in it, the breath of green living.

By twilight I can see the yearning grace of the red bat drinking in the midges. But it is night when the big brown bat lets himself down out of the zenith into lower darkness, only a deeper shadow. The last of the light drains back out of the west, runs again into the cup of day that is taken away from us.

By night birds sleep, except the owls. Squirrels sleep, but among the four-footed it is the immortal rule that the night shall belong to hunters. The mink comes up out of the river bottoms, poising a thoughtful paw and smelling the taints on the air.

A Prairie Grove

The bandit raccoon walks in the tree tops. Night is the waking time of the fox, and in the grass the meadow mice skip and chitter, and the deer mice, with dainty ears alert and small hearts pounding, go nimbly in their runways. Over their head the owl sweeps in a banked glide, his talons open.

This is the night as I know it, and I am safe in it. There is nothing anywhere, in all the length or the quiet depth of the grove, that I should fear, and nothing on the prairies. Across them I can see the orange pricks of light in the farmhouses, and when they wink away, and the shapes of the houses are only humps of darkness, there are stars. I am learning now to tell the time by them, by the great north road of the Dipper, and the crawling of the Scorpion across the black wall of the south. A sound, I find, will awaken the vesper sparrow—the gooselike cry of a car far off on the roads, or my own soft whistling to the high woods dripping their vines and their solemn freshness. Then the bird sings, a trill, a twirl, a reminder of life and day. Ask him any time, at any hour, and he will answer: we are here, song and I; we are only sleeping.

But the wilderness night was another world, and it was not gentle. There were big shapes in it; the gray wolf and the prairie wolf, the cougar and the

A Prairie Grove

lynx came alive with a yawn and a flexing of the claws out of the soft deception of fur, and began to hunger. It was all one hunger, the monarch hunger of the life forms that lie on the top of the vital pyramid, the few who may eat the flesh of the many, the strong who may tear the weak.

If the weak had a meaning, it was to satisfy the bellies of the strong. If the strong had a purpose, it was to keep down the lesser, to devour them in the folly of their running fertility. So the pyramid stood, each block of it having meaning only in relation to another. In itself no entity had inborn purpose. Of the purpose of the whole of that pyramid, never inquire, lest the answer, when you find it, make you afraid.

Somewhere in this great pyramid was wedged the block of man. Consider him, in his nakedness. He had but two feet with which to run, instead of four. He had no armor and no shell, and in his body no poison fangs, no sting. There was no check to his fertility but the check of death, swift or slow. He came into the world helpless, a dependent weakling longer than any other mammal's young. He was not, biologically, the mightiest block of the pyramid. But he could alter. He had dreams. And what he dreamed, it was his duty to make come to pass.

A Prairie Grove

There have been many dreams. There are dreams upon all the continents, and they are as ancient as the anthropoid skull in which they are entertained. I do not know what was dreamed beside the Niger; perhaps voodoo is a dream; nirvana is a dream of Asia; expectation of a harshly just heaven overarched the Nile. By the Congo, by the Brahmaputra and the Ho, there was no dream of change. Only Europe is restless, and will pull down its gods and put its fingers to new clay.

They say, in India, that the West is materialistic in its vision. The black man knows that the North is a slave raider, a white colossus stroking a lash in the hand. The red man gave to us, and in return we stole from him. The American wilderness, erect and unsuspecting, received us among its boughs and grasses, and we set an ax to it, and tortured it by fire. We have a black record; we are children who have struck at the breast that suckled us.

Now we bestride the top of the pyramid. Now we are great, now we are grown. Now we must find our own way, fend for ourselves. If we fall nobody will miss us. The pyramid will shape a new top; it will not be truncated; presently it will not remember. Now we have rebuilt, and I hope that we like it.

We have taken the terror out of the night. We have taken the checks from the lowly, the many with

A Prairie Grove

the little rodent teeth that work all night at their trade. We have softened everything, and how agreeable is our life!

In the cities, in the hospitals, our lights burn the night long, beside the writhing or the just breathing. There are nurses coming and going, bringing powders and chemicals; white-gowned doctors concentrate the rays that penetrate the flesh. By the police sergeant's desk the light is burning, the telephone is waiting; in the fire station the tongue hangs expectant over the gong. In the *yoshiwara* the devouring maladies wait in the bodies of the profaned, to devour the bodies that crawl smirking to them. In the laboratory behind locked doors the maker of gases prepares the death of civilians in the next war. The bankrupt thief struggles past midnight with the skein of strangling figures; the criminal's lawyer smells a hole in the law just big enough to let out a verminous rat. The childless woman weeps on the bed for her miscarriages. The young minister stares at his hands that can no longer pray in sincerity.

No, there are no terrors now in the night like the night terrors of the wilderness. No pack is after us, no fang is at our throats. We are a great people and a right people, and we live in the midst of plenty. And to those crying in the night it does no good to say, "It was our dreams that brought us all to this."

13

I AM NOT scoffing at our dreams. I respect them. It is against some prejudice that I bring myself to speak of the Indians' dreams—the actual nocturnal fantasies of the mind—yet I try to respect these too. The Indians went apart to have their dreams, to obtain a vision. Like first-century Christians they lived in huts, caves, solitary confinement, abstaining from food, from woman, from bathing, from exercise. Dirty, starved, wild-eyed and fanatic, they became at such times holy men. Saint Paul or Saint Augustine would have understood them more easily than could Father Prud'homme or the minister of a fashionable church. Is it just possible that Indians would have responded more favorably to first-century Christianity? But instead of the bodily stoicism, the fanaticism, the democracy and direct personal revelation of our religion in Roman times, they were offered the dream of Father Prud'homme.

Like most churchly officials, he was primarily absorbed by the task of spreading authority. He assumed that in heaven the popes and the recognized

A Prairie Grove

saints would be found clustered nearest the throne of God. He did not in the bottom of his heart believe in present-day revelation; miracle was a thing of history; it was something now to be taught to the docile. Like some modern missionaries, he was proudest of the quantity of his converts; he did not care whether they came for a bead or diversion, if in the end they found salvation. Fundamentally he could not really imagine them in Heaven; what he imagined was this dreadful wilderness dotted with church spires, the vibrations of the mission bells touching each other across the barbarous miles. He could see in a vision these people, their nakedness clothed, their spirits humbled, bringing their venison and their babies on their backs to the mission gates.

I am still wary of my prejudices, and I am striving hard for the moment to believe in the religious Pax Romana. When I think of Father Marquette, of Father Forreste, I am near to faith in it. Such men preached the brotherhood of man, and that dream, though it has never yet succeeded, has not failed us. I know of no other dream to trust. I could not trust any government always to be right; I do not trust the bankers or the economists or the military or my own judgment. I have some faith in science and art, because when they are pure they have no nationality,

A Prairie Grove

no hatreds, no greedy purpose. But I do not suppose that Plato would have made a successful executive, and in our polity there have to be executives. The ability to govern is a gift by itself, but even that gift is not enough. (Alexander the Great possessed it, though he was a moral deformity.) There must be added some towering honesty that would make the leader turn and chastise his children when they did wrong to others. We need that noble humor that is tolerance, and some proportion in the issues of the moment that will regard rather the great and the wide good of the future. The leader creates the future; what he dreams it is his duty to make come to pass.

To this description the Christian ideal answers well, but there has never been a body of churchmen that could be trusted with the management of all our affairs. One great saint in a generation is exceptional; it might be enough, if we could count on him. And remark that Christ and Buddha, Joan and Luther went ways outside the churches into which they had been born. Lincoln, Asoka, and Pasteur did what they did without churchly office. The dream of Father Prud'homme had every opportunity in the thirteenth century to bring about heaven upon earth.

A Prairie Grove

But as long as you believe in the Devil, you cannot exorcise him.

The dream of Robert Du Gay was a simple thing. It was explorative, exploitive, cloaked with politics, adorned with glory. Nothing could be easier for an American to understand. Commodore Perry knocking at the doors of Japan for trade, Roosevelt driving the Panama Canal through the rights and the inertia of a sister republic, the empire of Standard Oil—these are based on ideals like Du Gay's. It is not only an American ideal, though Europeans are fond of saying so; remember that Christopher Columbus, when he landed first in what he took to be the territory of the Great Mogul of India, immediately claimed it for the man who hired him, Ferdinand of Spain. The European temperament claims the best of everything, and never fails to add thereto the best of moral reasons for getting it. In this respect political empire is more hypocritical than commercial empire.

New France, as a political dream, was utterly shadowy and brief. Its claims were vainglorious, unsecured. Du Gay could discover a river five hundred miles in advance of any other white man, and could wave his sword at all that lay beyond and call it French, but he had no colonists behind him. The best Frenchmen will seldom leave France, and the gov-

A Prairie Grove

ernment had no wish to see them depart. Instead, it emptied the jails and took the base or bankrupt and sent them to new shores. By the St. Lawrence these unwilling colonists felt no temptation to build up civilization; instead, the birds whistled to them, and the tracks of the marten and fisher showed them the way deeper into the forest. The government had to pass a law compelling its Canadian subjects to cut down a certain number of trees every year; it tried to send wives out to them, but the *voyageur* was only too often already vanished into a world where French women could not live. He was brave; he was, I think, the most thorough and important explorer on the continent; he was hardy, adaptable, and a better friend to the Indian than anyone else. But he was the opposite of a colonist. In the wake of his canoe the waters swiftly closed again. He has left no memorials of himself that are tangible; he had no capacity for creation or foundation. One hundred and fifty years after Du Gay's time, the American Fur Company, a great net at the center of which in New York crouched John Jacob Astor, still preferred the *engagé*, as he was called, because he was subservient, unambitious, and never thought for himself.

To Robert Du Gay the resources of the land were not conceivably finite. He trusted to the vast fertility,

A Prairie Grove

the spawning numbers of the quadruped horde. No one will ever know, now, how great was the wealth in peltry in his day. In 1816 this state of Illinois still exported ten thousand deerskin, three hundred black bear, ten thousand raccoon, of muskrat hides thirty-five thousand, and of otter four hundred. Beaver and fox, mink and wildcat were then the small change of the trade. To this one must add the elk and bison of the century of Du Gay, when the running things were not yet in flight. The primeval fauna of the Great Basin from the Appalachians to the Rockies was then a wealth untouched; it stamped in red-eyed herds and it bounded, scarcely frightened, from any watering hole.

They are so gone now, the great beasts, that we have no sense of them left. We do not know enough of them now even to miss them. The sportsman goes, if he has the craving for big game, to Africa to hunt. But there was no sense of sport in the heart of Du Gay. It was too early in the morning of this land for that. Here in the great spread palm of the continent ran the animal world; they ate from that palm, they slept in it and rolled in it, and left, at last, their big hollow-eyed skulls in it.

Great bestial world. World of the gleaming fur changing with the seasons, beautiful intimate cloth-

A Prairie Grove

ing that is such modest nakedness. World of the many individual smells upon the grass and the ground and the air, imperceptible to us, signals of danger to the herbivores, promise of kill to the clawed. The beasts hunted in all places, knew all the runways, tried and tasted all that was good for them. And yet they despoiled nothing, scarcely broke the grass they walked through. Only the standing bear left his mark upon a chosen tree, and the beavers changed the look of rivers, making lakes of them that held reflections and amplified silence.

Yes, here they lived; they were foaled and dropped here and got to their shaking young legs, or they were littered in a den of good rank smells and warmth of fur and single desire for the teat. Then they ran, by day or by night, as the law told them, and they ate and they dropped back to earth its mineral fertility, their eyes glazed with the preoccupation of a rite. In the fullness of their time they knew the hunting or the howling agony of rut, a proud agony half pleasure, and they played their panting part in their race, without knowing what they did or remembering afterward what had become of their hunger. Then at the last there was the laboring breath, the staggering gait, darkness dripping over the vision. And finally, to stab them back again

A Prairie Grove

to one more moment of living, a last ecstasy of pain when the fangs went in and the spine or the skull was broken.

This was the million-lived life; this was the great North American faunal province, never so rich, so varied as where the elk looked westward out of the woods across the prairies, and the little sleek pocket gophers of this steppe met the straight proud wall of the oaks. Here the marten from Canada paused in the treetops with the fox squirrel hanging in his jaws, and the cougar, out of the south, sneezed dubiously at the tang of north upon the air.

The red man had no horse to chase them then. He had no gun, and in his hardihood could walk naked in the wind. Furs were for babies, for ceremonies, only in the worst of weather for protection. He had not learned yet that they could be turned into whiskey and powder, cotton cloth, steel axes, and vanity. Neither the Indian nor the beaver had ever heard of the beaver hat; Du Gay could buy cheaply what he might sell dear. The ermine of distant kings was only the weasel in his white winter pelage.

This man, this restless sleeper in the forest night, lying with his hand on his sword beside him, was not destined to grow rich, to rule, to have a queen. And New France was not fated to endure. The wind that

A Prairie Grove

held the white flag powdered with the golden fleur-de-lis died with a sigh beneath its folds. But the white man was dreaming his dream none the less; the seeds were falling secretly from his baggage, were blowing on the winds that favored him.

Now the beasts are slain; we are clothed, we are adorned. Now the submissive heifer is routed through the Chicago stockyards; mechanically it becomes beef and leather and glue. Now the sheep are choking beside the empty arroyo in the overgrazed lands; now the little man on the cheap street marks down the furs in his window—cat and rabbitskins dyed to look nobler, or shedding summer pelage smuggled out of Canada to evade the duty, the laws enacted to protect what we no longer have.

Do you want back Eden? But there was no dream in it but the vision of the midewiwin. There was no compassion beyond the family or the tribe. There was no help in suffering. You could not have the grand courageous schedule of the mail plane in the night going over the farm roof in the storm. Nor the Brahms First marching triumphant through the airs into a million hearts. You cannot have it both ways. You cannot call yourself a man and be willing to go back to the wolf's way. Our way has gone forth everywhere. Let me go on with the story of how it came to the island grove.

14

There were ears in that wilderness to hear everything, and every significant sound sent the peaked and furry skin forward to cup it. Everything listened, night and day, and a sound would break through nervous sleep where a smell might not.

A doe amidst the shield fern slept uneasily this night. There were sounds, and her wakeful ears bestirred themselves to orient them. Some part of her brain beneath the delicate skull sorted out the nature of these messages, and to the great gong of the will said, "Be still, be asleep."

So her heart was quiet. In the sweet summer doldrums, without thought she existed in the animal vegetative state. The autumn heat was far away; it was not foreseen. In this warm sleep peace dwells much of the animal world all the time. They are not forever fighting or fearing; they like to rest, they like to lie down, and only a blind man or a mechanist would deny that the animals like certain views. They can contemplate without having ideas about what they see. Do they see all the better for that?

But when a noise came the long ears cried out

A Prairie Grove

upon the consciousness; the doe rose on her brittle knees, and a light through the forest pricked her vision. Then she bounded up; the legs trembled and her tail stood out, the white hairs upon the rump erected. And now the taint of man flesh curled into her nostrils. She picked one forefoot up, and she stood long moments; more than fear was in her head. The light crooked a finger at her; it was like the incarnation of some manitou, it was spirit, magic, a challenge greater than danger. It flashed back from the inky balls of her eyes in the night, and very carefully she put that foot down. Then she began to walk forward in the fern, her long neck stretched. At her back she felt the darkness and the safety; ahead of her, cried every instinct, was only danger. But curiosity is not an instinct; it is a growing tip of the intelligence, it is a divinity upon the darkling animal mind, like the upward yearning of a vine toward sunlight. Courage and wonder together have carried us out of the night of our instincts toward the worship and the peril of our fires.

Around the small, the secret council fire sat a dozen of the Illinois in parley with their six Miami guests. The Miamis had spent a half day hidden in the next island grove to the east; they had sent a woman into the Illinois village with a secret message and a

A Prairie Grove

present of tobacco. And the old chief Nikanapi, knowing that in a few hours he would be hearing black words against the Frenchmen, had presented to his white guests all that afternoon the face of a smiling image. Now at the tip of the island, far from the sleeping Du Gay, he made his brothers welcome. What had the great Oumaha to say to the Illinois, that he had journeyed so far to see them?

Oumaha was not an old chief; he was, as only an Indian can be, both fat and hard. He got to his feet like a bull getting up, and first he showed his presents. He had axes and hatchets of tempered steel, copper kettles, red cloth, a burning glass, and rum. He asked them to know by these presents that he bore the Illinois the love of brotherhood. For their sakes purely he had come thus far to warn them. Strangers, he learned, had come among them, men who ate their food and plotted only treachery. These Frenchmen were in league with Iroquois; they were carrying guns and powder to the Sioux. With these two hands of their enemies, the Illinois and the Miamis would be strangled. The French had not yet the strength to do it themselves; they would buy Indians to do it for them.

"Brothers, they are few in your camp, and we are many. But the day will come when these invaders

A Prairie Grove

will grow like the grass stems, and you will be driven away like the buffalo before the prairie fires. Brothers, we have not misled you. Our gifts speak to you. We have no cause but yours. Now we will depart in peace as we came."

The lids of the listening Nikanapi fell guilelessly. Nothing, however, had escaped him; he guessed where the gifts had come from; he knew that they had cost Oumaha nothing, and that those were foreign words in Oumaha's mouth. If the Miamis had felt able to prove their assertions, they would have spoken them like men to the Frenchmen's faces; they would not have made haste to steal away in the night.

Yet he had never trusted the Frenchmen either, except Father Forreste. They had something to gain, or they would not be here. The hope of gain upon his own part precisely and delicately balanced the cost and the dangers of entertaining these imperious guests. The words of Oumaha and his gifts from the unseen white men behind him had tipped the scale, and he perceived that the treachery between white tribes might of itself be further profitable to him. This powwow was indeed a parry and thrust between two European nations. England had heard that Du Gay had gone to the Illinois country and, itself not

A Prairie Grove

ready to penetrate so far, wanted to play dog in the rich manger. The old chief, for his part, did not in the least believe that the white men could ever grow numerous as the grasses. There were not that many humans in the world, and this pale soft flesh was not the stuff of which warriors are made.

When his guests had gone, he told his listeners to say nothing of this to anyone. They must watch, on their guard, without changing face. Then the campfire was covered with earth, and leaves and twigs were laid on top of it.

The light had gone out in the forest, and the doe bounded away for a few paces. Then she walked more quietly, and she saw that the day was coming now in the east, and the night with its treacheries was over. She browsed from the trees, lifting the white of her chin to fumble and pluck among the leaves. Then she stepped deliberately back a little way along her tracks, bounded to one side, and found a fresh bed among the wood grasses that from their tussocks fling their green hair forward. Here she finished out her sleep, while the forest grew colored again and the long low sun shafts came to pierce it. They found her ears and shone through them, making a scarlet mesh of all the veins, and slipped in sheets of soft glory from the burnished summer coat of bay.

15

But the Sieur Robert Du Gay was no man's fool, and the Indian face could be read by shrewd experience. The Indian front was not united, and an hour after the French commander had first observed the sullen faces of his hosts, one of them, in the hope of reward, revealed the deliberations of the night before. Du Gay went straight to Nikanapi. He told the old man about a dream he had had, of how the Miamis, hired to the English, had intrigued against the great French father. A curious dream, was it not? And a false one, of course. Then he had had another dream; he had seen in a vision the arrival of his lieutenant, Rafael Pons, with thirty Frenchmen, muskets, and powder.

It was a long shot, but two days later the village was startled by the roar of guns, and the supporting party led by Pons swept through the parting curtains of the wilderness. The effect upon the Indians was astonishing. There was to them nothing finer in life than a dream come true, and nothing so much honored the dreamer.

A Prairie Grove

"We have listened to the whistling of bad birds," they said to one another, and their hospitality was redoubled as though it had never wearied. They were really eager to believe in their guests. Like children they asked that the knowing, mysterious beings among them and above them should be right and unbreakable. They hoped for good to come through them, and did not wish to be disappointed.

And the foreigners' eyes were so many mirrors in which the braves could see themselves. The dangerous and fascinating game of racial comparison could be played now upon this wilderness Field of the Cloth of Gold, with the proud swagger of kings and a hospitable waste of treasure. The bearded men and the affable girls measured racial ways of love and found the gestures strange and disturbing but the elements familiar.

Du Gay had so little interest in the effect that he produced among these unstable copper children that he scarcely stayed to notice it, and even his indifference made a mark. What impressed him was the rectilinear beauty of the European discipline. You could tell a man to meet you in the middle of the month, and on the fifteenth there he was. He would find you on an unmapped spot where he had never been before, though he had to cross a lake as wild as the North Sea and carry his boats on his back along the banks of rivers dwindled in the summer drought to muddy ditches.

Yes, it was a deep and a beautiful thing to look into eyes and know you would get a truthful answer; to see there belief and comprehension and clear thinking. The soldier's salute, the white man's handclasp, the rough, nervous embrace of a man friend— these were precious, but better still he loved the way Pons let the knowing laughter just glitter in his eyes, and the quick familiar idiom of his brows in comment. There was no treachery, no hysteria, no superstition about the man. He had the grace and the warmth of the south European, made upright by the habit of the trained soldier. And he took comradeship as much for granted as Du Gay himself. In the Iroquois wars Pons with five men had held Du Gay's line of retreat; he alone was the escaped survivor. And Du Gay, returned with a larger force, had hunted his lieutenant through the enemy's country, sacking the towns of the Five Nations, making them disgorge every prisoner, tracking his brother-in-arms as minutely as a lonely deer some doe remembered from an old autumn.

Sworn brotherhood was comprehensible to the Indians; it was a faith to them like the faith of lovers

A Prairie Grove

among us, more spiritual than the biological and physical bond of the family; a man who would give all for a squaw must indeed be far gone in sensual dementia. Among the Illinois the prestige of this unexpected friendship was immense.

The precious journal of Du Gay is a thing of clipped speech, elided emotions, and descriptions only in terms of resource. Of Rafael Pons the soldier I find nothing left but the maps that they carefully uncrease for me in the manuscript room of the historical society. The librarian watches me, not so much in fear for the documents as out of curiosity to see whether I will appreciate the faded and illegible treasure.

I like maps, and best of all I like them when they trace the unknown. That is where the man behind them looks out. I do not care whether he has estimated his distances precisely or put in all his rivers. What I look for is honesty—not to put in rivers he never saw, or fabled monsters he did not encounter. I like the sparsity of this Pons' map; he omits the trivial; he inscribes with the square calligraphy of the engineer. And this paper, this trustworthy witness of what once was, has the beauty of some leaf from Leonardo's sketchbook. It is the sketch for one shoulder of a continent, more exciting than the elaborate

A Prairie Grove

portrait finished in the studio. It has the sheer anatomy of geography, and it is true with the compass.

On that great simple chart is marked my island grove. He has marked it with some care, for he understood how easily it might be lost. You could pass it by, just over the brim of the horizon, to east or to west, and never raise it from the horizontal emptiness of the prairie. In the crooked creeks you could miss it, and flounder through the marshes with the reeds and bulrushes higher than your head. It had a way, the Indians knew, of drifting deep into perspective, when the haze of summer heat or of autumn fires made it a rootless phantom floating just above the grass heads. Then the cottonwood groves, with their talking leaves like squaws' tongues, and their deceptive height and whiteness, came out clear and false, and you might sweat through the marshes to get to them, only to find that they surmounted the back of no land, but ringed about hot shallow water and cakes of marl. And the frogs mocked at you, and the herons shot down white disgust upon you. But the true groves, with the dry grass and the open arms, could suddenly march a league nearer, in the glass-clear air when an October morning blew off sharp and bright.

So Pons pinned this portage place to reality, be-

A Prairie Grove

tween the stagnant Kilimick and, westward, the Seignelay, drowsing southward under its water lilies. They must have been in bloom that summer day when he and Du Gay walked over the ridge of the grove to look for a slight height proud enough to hold the flag of France, and the fort it should command.

16

IF Du Gay and Pons had told what they felt or described what grew high about them or peered at them around the boles of trees, they would not have been empire builders. Such men note only the details they need. There is no map of the island grove itself, and the best of the local historians have been out here looking for the site of the fort, without being able to locate it. For it was a mere palisade of tree trunks enclosing a log house adapted slightly to European methods of defense. As a precaution against Indian attack, the woods and brush were cleared in a wide swathe around the stockade. But the woods and brush have seen to that little matter, long since. These trees, so venerable to me, were acorns then that the fox squirrels had buried but forgotten.

But I feel a great longing to go back and stand in the clearing's sunlight with those Frenchmen. I want to look at precisely what they saw and feel as far away as they did. For there will never again be distance like theirs. The true measure of space is

A Prairie Grove

time; they were two months from Kébec, and you cannot now, except upon antarctic ice or in the Matto Grosso, get two months away from anything. They were six months from France, and what Colbert might say in a letter reached them as dead news, like the happenings among the stars. If indeed the letter ever found them. And if it did—why, here amidst the shagbarks, the wild American crows, the shifting human pack, here the vermilion boast of a minister's seal was nothing but wax. The writ of that brittle wafer did not run upon these sun-worshiping grasses. This west wind would not carry the king's messages. Du Gay and Pons, old soldiers, knew it; for all their loyalty to Louis and his flag, they knew they had to take initiatives; event was upon them, and they must bear themselves under the sky and before men like kings in their own right.

Something is still left in these woods and the beasts in them that does not want to learn what we have tried to teach them. This is a tall hard male nature, and it will not love you for beating it. It will not come crawling back, like the jungle, when you have cut it down. There is no bend in its knee; you have to raze it if you want wealth from the soil it claimed.

This biota has about it the scorn of man that was

A Prairie Grove

here before man found it. There is no gold in the earth, no precious latex in the trees, there are no annual grasses native to be sown for crops, and no healing quinine or fabled spice. Nature here does not promise man any extravagant gain; it has given him grudgingly a home and a living if he would work for them. Austere and economical of effect, intemperate of weather, it holds no softnesses and will not frame a view for you. Its beautiful designs are in the convolutions of the oak's knotwood, or in the arch of many grasses all one way and equal. It is not a flowering wilderness, but one of stems, trees, and grass. It has so much sky that the grass can never fill it, though it runs forever to reach the cup's brim. It talks with the bluejays' tongues; it used to beat with the cougar's heartbeat and die each year with the killing and feasting, the searing of the maize stalk, and the ragged southward streaking of the cranes in the Indian summer.

Were the hawthorns so many in my woods, in the days before they let in the cattle? Where did the barn swallows nest then, and the domestic chimney swifts? In the twilight dared the cottontails come out and sit palpitating, enjoying life for all its terrors? I tramp this grove trying to learn and remember the intricate chain of its vernal sloughs

A Prairie Grove

that pipe with tender batrachian song when the trillium makes constellations amidst the old stumps. I find and lose again great ash trees that are three-forked from the base; I can even discover now the doorway of that rarest of all our quadrupeds, the pine mouse, who passes a subterranean life gnawing the bark from the hawthorn roots. But I do not know in which glade swamped with moonlight the old black bear pawed a bed.

For there were bear here, the black bear who stood up on their hind legs and picked raspberries, turned over logs for beetles, grubbed out roots, nourished no rancors, were sleepy as bats, and could live on their own fat in lean times. Now only the children look for bear in these woods any more. They are on the long list of the vanished mammals, together with the neat marten, the beaver and otter, the elk and the deer and, on the prairies, the burrowers—the little pocket gophers and the big surly badgers. The great gray timber wolves have had to go; the lynx and the bobcat and the fisher I cannot even imagine now in the candor of these woods, far less the cougar.

But they were here in the days when the tall tree at the end of its years fell into the arms of some younger brother. Then there was timber, now we

A Prairie Grove

have only trees. For the big carnivores there must be rankness, unkempt and barbaric; they need a self-enclosed world of interlocking branches and a forest floor with so deep a pile that the dew lies heavy almost up to noon. The night belonged to them, and even in the long winters they could not sleep but hungrily ranged the shadows on the snow. In the world that was given to them at the creation of this country, they were as secure as they were needful. For now without them we have the plague of mice, the preposterous abundance of the cottontail. Nothing fateful is in the woods now, nothing very secret any more, no heavy paw to fall.

I make the most of such quadruped fauna as is left to us, and I suppose that only in a world lacking the long fangs and the heavy hooves would I come, curious and with every sense alert in me, to read tiny runes, to learn the ways of the meadow mice and the deer mice, and of the shrews, the smallest mammals in the world. One that I found dead last winter I lost in the snow, and I could not find him again until the thaw. Some other creature had been at him, and there was nothing left of him except a skull that I picked up at last after patient scrutiny; it was so thin that it felt like paper and the light shone through it. Alas, poor little

A Prairie Grove

Yorick! you will not dart out of your lurking place again upon the beetles turning the fallen oak to powder. You and your kind are all I have to muse upon; I can walk round and round the muddy prairie pond but I will not find the battle horns of a bull bison fallen at the wallow in the great autumn fights. Once in the fall of the year was the rutting season of the buffalo and elk and deer. Now no beasts, bleeding but triumphant, round up the does or cows. Only the bats mate nowadays in autumn, and when and how they do it I have never seen.

I walk out to the edge of the grove and stand there leaning on my white man's hand against the bark of a black oak, and I look west. But I do not see the sodden grassy might of the marshes; I do not see the sacred fields of the tobacco around which the Indians piled hedges of brushwood. When they had planted their crop they set this rood screen around a thing too holy to be seen. For this plant, the *petun*, and *mandamin* the maize were given them by the gods, the earth and the sun and the water.

I think sometimes that all things were given us by the gods, and I am not sure that under that law a man may own a flower or a tree, a bird, a beast,

A Prairie Grove

or a view. We may take life if we are going to use it for a need; that is, to make more life. But we are not the lords here; life itself is lord. Each of us, the tendril and the mouse, the man, the little she-bat sailing through the night like a witch with her baby clinging to her back—we cup the gift for a moment; we cannot keep it longer. The world's beauty and the five senses and the sweet well of sex and the strength to stand and the right to breathe are as holy as ever were the *petun* and the *mandamin*. And the day may come when, sick of our own follies, we shall recognize that what we claim in our pride to own is all an Indian gift.

17

THE TROUBLES between Father Prud'homme and Du Gay must have been gathering to the point of explosion all through July. It must have been, as much as anything, a matter of discordant personalities. Father Prud'homme protests so many times in his record that he was ready at every moment to lay down his life for the glory of God and that his only desire was to labor for the soul's salvation of the red man, that Du Gay finally took him at his word. If Prud'homme really wanted to store up treasure in heaven, he should go to the Sioux, the wildest hordes of the plains. They were the only other tribe of whom the Iroquois thought with respect. They had the horse now, the wild runaway from the Spaniards in the southwest; they had the short-grass plains to themselves, and they lived in a world of kill and hide and gorgeous featherwork, without those cowed humilities that infect the hearts of folk who know the mystery of forest. From afar they saw everything that could approach them, and had time to raise their hate. Stony sod indeed for the Christian seed!

A Prairie Grove

Prud'homme was not a hypocrite; he was startled, but he bowed his head to the challenge and went. Two Frenchmen accompanied him, and as they bent their backs to the paddle, he stiffened his own, and turned his face toward his duty, not expecting bodily mercy or that his God would upon the Judgment Day show mercy to those who might hear the Word and refuse it.

The hammers were still ringing upon the fort when on the eighteenth of August Du Gay, too, started south down the Seignelay, with twenty-five men. He had to act now to invalidate the claims of Spain upon the lower Mississippi. The Seignelay falls into the Father of Waters, and while Prud'homme went toward the source of the great river, he, Du Gay, must follow it to its mouth. Only so, when France could put her finger on the top of the map and the bottom and say her sons had planted her standard there and there, could she face down the King of Spain narrowing his lids and stroking his preposterous jaw in the morose Escorial.

If I were writing biography, I should tell the story of Du Gay and of Prud'homme. Their adventures were great enough for any book. But the island grove is my story; when he leaves my stage, I may not follow the actor. Du Gay, for his part, made a

A Prairie Grove

handsome exit. Pons, who was to remain with fifteen men, staged it with all the military form that he could muster. The Indians in full costume massed outside the fort in an effect of loyalty; the guns roared, the flag dipped. The startled waterfowl rose in farewell, crying away over the wild rice, and the wind fluttered the gold and scarlet cloak like a last laugh of courage. In the country of the Arkansas the great chevalier was to be murdered by his own men, and they in their turn meeting with just vengeance, that cloak thirty years later would be flung at the feet of the first French admiral to sail up the Mississippi from the sea.

And Prud'homme? He earned his heavenly prestige. Seven years after he left my island, there appeared at the gates of the mission of St. Ignace a twisted cripple in torn skins. His face was heavy with beard; he had the inhuman skin of an old Indian, and he spoke as though he hardly dared to utter the French language. But from under his buffalo tatters with the lice in them he drew out the chalice that the Sioux had been afraid to touch. The light from it flashed in his own eyes, and the Jesuits saw that though he had lost his reason he had not lost his faith.

Within the fort in the island grove, Fort Col-

A Prairie Grove

bert, Rafael Pons remained at his post that August. He had fifteen men at his command, and not one of them was a soldier. They had not even the bearing of soldiers, and there was no certainty that he could enforce the simplest sort of discipline. At night he was the only one who slept inside the palisade. By day half of them were out hunting to supply their own needs. God knew there was plenty of the wildfowl. You could get fifty ducks in an hour, but his men melted away for sport to escape the tedium of sentry go and barracks life. Pons had no guarantee from surprise attack. He could count upon his Indian allies just as long as intangible prestige personally surrounded him. He had the soldier's sensitiveness to the details of his *tenue*. To stumble on a log, to miss fire, to be seen in undress or sleeping—these were actual strategic false steps. Never look vulnerable, never appear undecided or reveal any plan or motive or surprise.

Time was against him, and he knew it. He might have to hold this position for two years. Peace might be as dangerous as war; it bred familiarity, relaxed the guard; it made the martial gestures empty. And already the great ennui of the wilderness had become a force. There seemed to be no wind any more to lift the flag; it shrank to its standard, and

A Prairie Grove

because there was no motion left in it, the French soldier had to set himself to a cadenced step, marching round and round the palisade.

The summer drought now showed its yellow face. The land that in spring stood four-fifths under water seemed half desertic now. First there was the smell of mud and stranded decay; then the mud opened in seismic cracks, and out of the coarse and to him nameless plants was baked the terebinthine smell of goldenrod and prairie dock. There was just a hint of tar about it, enough to make memory—more sensitive to odor than even to half a strain of melody—raise up Marseilles and the wharves. Marseilles was hot too, and this man's native Provence in summer shimmered and shrilled with the cicada-haunted golden dust. But there you had old wells under their roofs like little shrines, with maidenhair growing in the shadowed crannies down the shaft. You saw the flash of the scythes going through the grain, and men called from one hillside to another. A woman bending down to scoop a sheaf in a brown arm showed the half of each globed fruit under her vest. Through the olive trees shone the geometrical level of the Mediterranean.

Here in the depths of another continent there was no sea; here an unstable and excessive climate

A Prairie Grove

knew no medium between flood and drought. The rivers, the only highways of this land, were withered now till the children waded across them, and you could not have advanced or retreated by canoe if the fate of New France had depended on it.

Nothing seemed more alien to Pons than the absence of woman. In the squaws he recognized female humans, but there was nothing about one of them that went to make up that being, that experience, that home that is *la femme*. His heart was warmer than his absent commander's; he needed something to love, and there was nothing that needed him here. Only the flag needed him, and watching it by the hour and through the weeks he gave it the worship of his eyes.

At night he had the light of a fire, but there was no book to read by it, and it was not his way to keep a journal. What would he have written in it? Only the desertions, one at a time, two at a time, and another day without rain.

Father Forreste was a dying man, but he would not be brought inside the fort. Indian women had made him an arbor under wild grape. The last of the wine was gone, and he lay looking at the spindling pendants of the hard green American fruit, wondering if they would ripen before he died. He

A Prairie Grove

was lucid but remote; he was so filled with the coming wonder of the love of God that he required nothing of the love of man. When his fellow white man touched his hand it was always already cold, and there was nothing in the eyes that turned to the soldier's but a vast gentle darkness.

Pons did not fail to appreciate his countryman; he recognized discipline, devotion, and stoicism when he met them. But he had been too long a soldier to think of any speech he could bring to this fallen warrior of God. His recollection of priests was clearest from his childhood, when he went to confess that he had been guilty of the sin of gluttony, had disobeyed his mother and stolen from a baker's shop. Would he trouble now this passing soul with the confession that he had killed men, lied for his king, lain with a woman on his last night in Europe? There seemed to be no reality in sin this far from the cool church doorway, and this far in life from his mother's tender scolding. There was nothing but *tenue*, and there were no eyes but your own to hold you to it.

18

AT THE LAST, Father Gabriel became delirious. He talked, and the Illinois said to one another, "He is having a vision." A wise old man, a spirit on earth, was possessed of revelation. So they came and sat around his arbor to listen. They were rows deep, and nothing that Pons could do could drive them away or prevent them from crowding about the sick man. They had come to express their sympathy, they were doing him honor, and they might hear from him some message of the great Master of Life with whom he spoke. The medicine men were respectfully present; they entirely admitted him to a category above themselves, and the secrets of his bread and wine, his cup and his incantations had challenged and fascinated them. The whole village seemed suddenly to have nothing to do except gratify curiosity about the way in which this white spirit would depart this life. They seemed to Pons like monkeys, as they sat there eating and smoking, unconscious of the vermin upon them.

Within the darkened room of Forreste's conscious-

A Prairie Grove

ness the presence of these his children was only a vague disturbance among the shadows. He was troubled, too, by the intolerable heat of the day that clamped upon his forehead like aching bands. He smelled the tobacco smoke which he had always loathed, but he thought that he was a child sent to the tavern on an errand by his father, and as one odor supplies the memory of another that may be linked to it, he imagined the reek of the stale cheap wine and the drunken singing of a solitary old sot at whose expense all the others used to have jokes and laughs.

His parents had been peasants driven by economic forces to the cities. Here they took the lowest station above beggary, and subsisted just level with the dregs. As a child he came from the innocence of country to the noisy, knowing, and self-preservative life of the guttersnipe. He discovered then that, though the beast have no vices, even children may be beastly. He learned that there is no limit to how much a gang of boys can enjoy torturing something defenseless. He heard nasty words in the mouths of little girls, and discovered that whatever they had that you could call modesty about them might be nothing but precocious provocation. Above his head wrangled and suffered the grown-up hu-

A Prairie Grove

mans. He knew the bitterness of seeing his parents submissive before evictions; he saw through their pretenses when they were trying to impress some prospective landlord of their solvency. It seemed to him that the thin walls of the tenements of Rheims, Amiens, and Rouen must all be made of the same sandy plaster, for it was forever dribbling away. It grounded him thoroughly in the first lesson about material security, namely, that there is none. The thinness of those dingy walls taught him the soul's equality, for on the other side of them you could hear the strangling of the diphtheritic baby, the rising, raging voice of a woman getting ready to whip a child, the unconscious groans of a man too tired to sleep at peace. Above the roof tops, fantastic as some fructification pushed out by lichen, rose the Gothic spires of the cathedral.

The child Jacques—he had taken the name of Gabriel upon entering the order—was not shrinking; he was not an artist with a special gift to be sheltered. He had peasant strength and even gusto for life; he was not broken, not even deeply shocked by his experiences. He was bigger than the street boys of his age, and bigger than the city men when, a man, he went to work among them as a day laborer. But his convictions grew as sturdily as the great

A Prairie Grove

body that God had given him. And the priests presently began to notice him. There are not many men of twenty-two who come morning and evening, day after day, to pray in the darkness of the aisles, and what they could not read in the stained glass mystery was revealed in the blaze of sunlight on the porch steps of the cathedral. Already written in his face the priests saw what they had been promised in the seminary would come to them upon their ordination. So they made overtures to him; only then did they discover that he could not yet read or write.

But genuine humility and submission are cardinal virtues which the Church knows how to appreciate, though it could scarcely be expected to elect one of its great executives for such qualities. The call to the American mission field found the now educated and consecrated Father Gabriel a willing respondent, and among these bronze children of the wilderness he was not so far from the known and the forgivable as one who had been better born in this world and might die more ill prepared for the next. It was not strange to him that the Indians lied and stole by nature, nor that a hairsbreadth divided their friendship from their pitiless treachery. Not even wholly unfamiliar to him was the unspeakable torture he had once helplessly witnessed, followed by

A Prairie Grove

a village saturnalia which sent him sorrowfully away alone into the dark forest to pray.

Now he was entering for all time the dark and the unexplored. But he was not afraid. He thought how first God made the world and all that in it is; He made the sweet land of France, He made the cool shadows of its trees and the flocks of sheep, the many, many sheep running and bleating after the shepherd. He made the dark might of the ocean marching and marching by its white-topped combing waves. And He made the new-found world holding the gift of the five Great Lakes with their pure deep saltless water. He gave to this land its river sycamores so generous of girth that in the hollow ones you could have stabled two horses; He planted out the pasturage of the prairies. In both countries He was found; He was always in the sky which is indivisible and arches impartially over the nations. God waits for His children to come to Him, and it is no farther to Him from the western wilderness than from one's own threshold in Normandy.

Father Gabriel did not know it, but he was speaking his thoughts. He struggled up and opened his eyes, and the arm of Rafael Pons went beneath his shoulder blades. The blue of the drought sky filled his eyes, and he thought that he was kneeling at the

A Prairie Grove

hem of the Holy Virgin's robe. "I see the sheep," he said, "the many, many sheep coming to the Shepherd." Then he died, with his head rolling forward on the captain's sturdy shoulder.

A cry of sympathy and respect ran through the Indian crowd. "What does he say?" they asked. "What is the vision of the spirit?" And they crowded insistently, suffocatingly, around the kneeling Pons who laid the old man down. He turned, and the soldier in him brought him to his feet. He was swept by a moment's sympathy with these savages who in the presence of death had the universal human hungering to know what lies beyond, and he spoke to them in their own language and answered their own need:

"He said that he saw the great Master of Life, who was sending buffalo, many, many buffalo."

The deep-throated word of approval came out of all the strong bare chests. "Hau!" they said, like talking crows. "Hau! It is a good vision. He has indeed spoken with the Master of Life."

Pons had dreaded that the savages would take the Franciscan's funeral out of his hands. He did not want even their grief, knowing the highly histrionic nature of it; he had seen a man walk into the midst of his own obsequies, when he had been

A Prairie Grove

long missing, and being full of Dutch whiskey, sit down with his relatives and weep for himself for two days. But to his surprise, the Indians were too genuine in their sorrow to wail. They came to him and asked him if it were not time now to ring the little bell. They were never so delighted as when the priest had rung the little altar bell at mass; the meaning of this ceremony was utterly opaque to them, but there were some who had come to mass chiefly to listen for the unpredictable moment when the sound of the small brass bell struck across the piping of the frogs or the gobbling of the wild turkeys. They supposed that by its means he aroused the attention of a drowsy manitou.

Already the young men had made a coffin of two boats; women had dug a trench so deep that the coyotes would never find the bones. They understood that it was not the custom for the white men to paint their faces, alive or dead; the last gift to him of their vermilion and walnut stain they had denied themselves.

So now they made ready to double the thin old body into the position it had held in the womb. Tactfully Pons showed them how the white men lay out their dead. "You see, it is like a great tree that falls down unbroken. When the Master of Life

A Prairie Grove

upon the last day of the world shall call His good children to come and feast with Him forever in the skies, they will rise from this position right up on their feet."

They let the coffin down into the trench with ropes of wild hemp as Pons showed them how to do. Then the five remaining Frenchmen knelt and muttered the prayers they could remember. Pons crossed himself and bowed his head; the black generous earth flung back by women's hands rattled on the top of the coffin; Nikanapi rang and rang the little bell. On the burning prairie the field sparrows heard it and after a pause of listening they answered it with their sudden overflowing rapture.

19

It is an old miracle how spring will come back in spite of snow and sorrow and war. But in other lands than ours one cannot say much for autumn, except that there must be an end to all things. In temperate North America, in the hardwood forest belt, it is autumn that triumphs over drought and summer weariness; it sweeps in with the sense of freshening, of a new coming to life and an actual reawakening of the instincts.

There was in the wilderness days a whole great biological pulsation that was autumnal. The prairies then filled with grass herbage like a rising lake. Ankle-deep and starred with little wildflowers in the spring, it rose above a man's head in the fall. It was gorgeous with the purple spikes of blazing star and the gold of the sunflowers. The big grasses flowered in autumn, and when the green began to go the bronzes came, the tawnies like the wildcat's fur, the low-toned, burned-out vermilions like old war paint. And then at last, when the squaws had pulled the corn ears and the children, with the little

A Prairie Grove

melon bellies, had dutifully rolled the pumpkins to warm another side in softening sunlight, the prairie suddenly died. Color drained out of it like light from the top of the evening sky. And then the tumult in the island groves began.

Part of it was crows, a clan of birds that is shocked by everything, and part of it was the flight of the does, who do not come to heat so soon as the bucks. They crashed through the forest with eyes starting and exultant, knowing the rapture of flight from a pursuit that meant no harm to them. They say that a buck would follow one doe who would elude him by running among her sisters, crossing her scent with theirs; then he would drive the pack of them, rearing and bounding, divide it and quarter it and scatter it, trying to find his first desire and losing himself in a maze of scents, all of them female and all of them now dissipated upon the sudden fresh wash of the north wind through the softly applauding forest. Then his neck would swell with passion; he would throw up his head with his nostrils flaring and his antlers tossing the sumach leaves, the surroyal tines clattering the dead black twigs of the hickory boughs. After weeks of such pursuit, his body wasted with running and fighting his rivals, this torment-ridden fury discovered all at once that the

A Prairie Grove

does were wraiths no longer. They were suddenly still in their tracks, fine legs trembling, dark dilating eyes turned back toward him; in the calm steeping sunlight the perfume of these gentling friends washed back to him, bathed him and promised kindness; the scarlet and the orange and the gold of the leaves rained through the antlers and drifted about the motionless black hooves.

For the autumn colors were part of the tumult. There is no other land in the world with autumns like ours. We pile the treasure of the year into a great burial fire. Tongues of flame go up to the sky, the garnet of black and red oaks, the leaping maples and the flickering aspens and out of the midst of it all one exulting spire of light where a cottonwood shakes primal yellow at the primal blue of the American sky. From the boughs pours down the glory of the vines—woodbine and corded grape and poison ivy. The thickets fill with the cymbal colors of the sumach—orange and scarlet and stain of wine; the leaning dwarf forest of the hawthorns begins to drop its shower of little pomes—ruby color overcast with purple bloom. They tumble in a circle, a wild harvest no less bounteous because only mice and children gather of it. Under the trees curls the violet breath of the asters. And still sometimes,

A Prairie Grove

where the cattle have not trampled, I find a lonely gentian hoarding blue. It keeps its corollas closed against the bee, dropping pollen from the linked brotherhood of the anthers upon the stigma, like some divinely descended royalty that must propagate within its own sacred circle.

The jays, blue crows that they are, have much to say in autumn, and they talk as though they remembered the clamor of the old abundance. For those were the days when upon the dwindled river marshes already crowded with wildfowl, the hordes from the north descended. The redwings devoured the wild rice; they rose in irritable black tempests when the Indians came among them, bending the freighted heads of the rice over their canoes, beating the grains into skins spread waiting on the boat bottoms. The yellowlegs and the plovers came back then, teetering, piping, foraging at a run upon the mud. The wild geese went over, high, too high for the upward rain of arrows. The great cranes felt the disconsolation of shortening days, and began to stream away—mere etched lines of gray on the soft gray plumage of a sky promising moisture and the break of drought.

They say the cougar mated in the fall, but he is more vanished now than the credible memory of

A Prairie Grove

the elk. King of the antlered kind, the elk in the great rutting season was a creature of terror. Nocturnal then, his fights were like the matching of Sioux strength with Iroquois. Rousing himself out of the mud wallow where he had retreated from the stings of the horseflies, the old master of the herd stumbled up, blew out his matted nostrils, and began to remember the number of his does. He rounded them together, perhaps a score of them, with a warning scream of his perpetually impending displeasure.

When they strayed, he struck at them unmercifully, for he smelled other bucks upon the air. He knew that some of the young does of the year had already eluded him and got to the gatherings of the males. Already there were minor passages at antlers, for the possession of these escapes. But these does were too few for the increasing herd of hunting males, and they followed up the wind to the old one's chivied wives.

So he must turn, and in the moonlight show in a hideous grin his hatred of those younger males that gathered in a waiting, wavering row, their hindquarters deep in the pool of forest darkness and the safety of retreat.

Then a challenger would step forward and bring

A Prairie Grove

his muzzle down to the luscious river of doe scent on the grass. The prongs of his antlers pointed then directly at his foe. They were twice as terrible as the buck deer's, branched like the snagged tree that tears the bottom out of a shooting canoe, and between the mighty arches of the shafts sprouted the two brow tines and the two bez tines. These were the weapons of the close attack, and the moonlight sharpened them dangerously.

The scream of the challenger was answered by the down thundering of the old Turk's charge. They met with a crash and a shock that sent the other rivals scattering, plunging, snorting away in the greater desire of escape. There was a sound of the snapping of the slenderer tines, and the harsh wrangling of the locked branches. They swayed and pushed and panted, and the does looked back from their cropping with the soft eyes of the enslaved. The old lord found some second strength; he began to thrust his enemy—his own son—back with a measured merciless science. The young buck reared back for the breakaway and found that his tines were snagged in his conqueror's. The fighters sensed their mutual danger; they rolled their heads in one frantic futile purpose. The fight staggered and crashed into the darkness, and the young bucks came back, and

A Prairie Grove

snorting and screaming they cut the harem this way and that, driving off the does by fours and fives and sixes, stopping to battle with each other and losing their favorites to a third. So under the eyes of a moon sagging in harvest orange toward the west, the wild irregular mating went on and was repeated on the next night, and the next, until the old lord and his challenger staggered dead in the forest and the young bucks, spent with their revels, sick of them, ravenous for grass, left the does some peace at last, left them to follow, chained now by the unrebellion of their new state.

In the autumn, after the death of Father Forreste, the Indians waited in confidence for the coming of the many buffalo. They had not been sighted all through their mating season of August and early September, and late September came, and still there were no buffalo. The river was swarming with waterfowl; the deer and the elk were hunted, and young boys brought in bobcats and lynxes, opossums and raccoons. The turkeys fattened till the old gobblers were as heavy as a child of five. The little teal were so full-fed that when they fell upon hard ground they burst. Throughout the Illinois village there was one great skinning and roasting and a running of grease and fat. There were hides to scrape and

A Prairie Grove

bags of fur to be sewn and dyed yellow with the bark from the oak and black with the walnut stain and scarlet with the redroot. There was a cutting of robes out of elk skin and deerskin and a shaping of moccasins, and among the rushes the women prodded for the ripened tubers of the arrowhead and the lotus, robbing the muskrats of next winter's food.

Now there was corn again, and bear's grease for the hair, and wildcat oil to rub on the tired leg muscles. The girls were sent to cut rushes for mats and baskets, pouches and thatching, and they felt free there and called to each other through the lisping forest of the marsh stands; they chattered and idled, because the sky was so blue and tranquil you could not believe in the winter coming. A young bittern in his first striped autumn plumage was caught asleep standing there so slim with his beak pointing upward that he looked like a reed; one girl wandering away from the rest came on him, seized him by the neck and carried him back, laughing, with his wings beating around her shoulders. That year a male fawn had shot right into her arms; now the girls asked her when she was going to catch a man. She tossed the bittern free with a laugh. "When the buffalo come back," she said, and they

A Prairie Grove

understood her. For the buffalo and the *coureurs* were bearded.

The Illinois were relieved now of their guests. A message had come from Michilimackinac that all Canada was harried by the Iroquois, and the captain Pons had tried to rouse his Indian allies to the defense of New France. But Nikanapi had replied that the Illinois went to war in February; now the buffalo, many, many buffalo, had been promised to them by the white spirit. When Pons turned back, the remaining five *coureurs* at the last moment sobered and came to him, and with the first fall of the autumn torrents the six aliens had vanished down the Kilimick.

The fort was empty now, and the flag was gone, but the Indians liked to wander in it, full of amazement and some little scorn for so much hollow effort. It made them all laugh when one of them would sit down on a rude chair like a white man or pretend to write a message or salute. There were gifts of the white man's clothing left in the village, and Nikanapi was proud to put on a cavalier's hat with a curled and drooping plume. Several of the women had received garments too, but the men took them away and wore them without any loss of dignity among their kind. By next spring these che-

A Prairie Grove

mises and petticoats would be too dirty to wear outside the body, and they would be carried under the ceremonial robes until, their donors forgotten, they were flung rotted away.

The white oaks were naked and the red oaks, clinging to their leaves, were faded to the color of dried tobacco, when the village roused up to the cry of *"Pisikiou!"* They pounded to the edge of the grove and saw on the western horizon the toppling column of dust that was the buffalo, and nearer at hand, staring at the eastern wall of the woods, the vanguard of the cows, alert to all that the wind brought them of danger out of the woods.

20

No one will ever know within two or three million the numbers of the bison horde. When the creature was going, stumbling toward extinction, there were censuses.

You come on phrases, from Texas, from Wyoming, serious estimates: "About a million"; "only half a million now"; "twenty-five thousand." The greatest North American animal of historic times, it stamped from the eastern forests to the Rockies, it wandered north in summer up to Athabaska and struggled through the drifts with the norther at its hindquarters into Texas. When the bison went on the march to the salt licks of Kentucky, to the watering holes of the great plains, it traveled sometimes in single file. So the buffalo trails were made. These were the first roads that ever crossed the continent. The Indians walked in these trails too, as a goshawk will stalk down a rabbit's runway through the brush. The white men followed in the buffalo way, and they called it "the buffalo trace," "the Kentucky road," "the Governor's trace." Cutting

A Prairie Grove

through the tedium of rectilinear Chicago today runs the slanting Vincennes road; here the buffalo came from Indiana to the prairies. They were monarchs once, thundering along the routes where now the trucks and busses rattle on the metaled highways.

All but two of the continents have had their buffalo or their wild oxen, and there are most of them in Asia. In the rice fields of India plod the water buffalo, subdued to the will of the children that tend them. The cliff paintings of the European New Stone Age show impounded herds of long-horned cattle, and there is a memory in Russia and the marshlands of Lithuania of the aurochs that stood as tall as the American bison. But it had not the mighty chest of our plains monarch. For the bison, like the lion, was a king in front; he had the eye of wrath, the snort of scorn, the collar of kingship; only in the hinder quarters did he betray how he too was mortal flesh. At the height of the hump a bull stood six feet, a cow a foot less. A full-grown master of the herd would measure nine feet from the muzzle to the rump. When he stamped, he could throw the weight of a thousand pounds upon whatever lay beneath his feet. The horns of the bison curved upward, fit for battle. Among the American fossil species there are some whose horns stand out

A Prairie Grove

at right angles, and others with drooping horns. Only the one combative, prolific, indomitable sort survived the glaciers.

The last of the buffalo were wary, but the great original horde relied upon the might and the temper and the collective will of the mob which, be it buffaloes or ants or angry men, leaves the individual slight choice and a drunken insensibility to details and warnings. Perhaps there were many herds, or perhaps, biologically speaking, it was one great population. Where it went, grinding the grass with the many million molars and covering the land with the returned fertility of its great flaps, the horseflies swarmed and gorged themselves; the cowbirds walked among the great beasts, sat on them and ate their ticks and lived themselves in polygamous, helpful, jackal plenty. The wolves hung on the flanks of the herd, gray flickering cowardice emboldened by hunger. A strong cow defending her calf would stamp them out like tongues of prairie flame; a bull would toss them gored from his horns into their own ranks to be devoured. One of the old cattle could stand them off for a day; in the end they got him, and the hungry waves closed over him.

Wherever the herd turned they had the Indians

A Prairie Grove

upon their trail. The Crees and the Arickarees, the Mandans and Kansas, the Ioways and Osages lived by the buffalo. They lusted for him as the wolves did, but with that strange human element in lust called love. They worshiped what they killed; they feasted on his flesh and they wore his horns because it gave them stature. Of his bones they made their ladles and bodkins; they used his sinews for thread and his dung for fire. Their wigwams were of buffalo hide, so were their boats and robes and moccasins and belts. Even the Illinois learned from the Sioux to make a shield of buffalo leather, and the Illinois women spun the buffalo wool, sometimes as fine as silk, for gowns sewn with roebuck sinews, for garters, belts, and dyed scarves. The buffalo meant abundance, warmth, excitement, and when they came it was as if earth had suddenly flung open the woolly sack of plenty and given wealth and purpose. They put the manhood into man, they gave him his way of life; they were what he could win by bravery. His art and his songs, his prayers and his dances exulted in the perilous opportunity that thundered on him in a golden pillar of dust.

Trampling eastward from the western droughts, from the harrying of the mounted Sioux, came the buffalo to the prairie seas about my island grove.

A Prairie Grove

They had the wind against them, and they could not smell the Illinois encampment, but they saw the woods and they flanked away to southward. In the shadows of the trees Nikanapi held the young men back. He did not want the wary cows started with a premature attack. And a buffalo surround was a half religious matter, not to be entered on without some thoughts and reverence for this fellow creature who was friend and enemy. It gave the chief the opportunity he never neglected for oratory and the bestowing of advice. So he told them all what they all knew already, but being ceremonious animals, they liked to hear it again.

The attack was planned like a battle, and the first war party was sent behind the groves and in the concealing marshes far ahead to start the prairie fire. On the flank of the herd the village waited, hidden, watching the great straggling defile till the center with the calves went by, and in the rear, ready with fire, the most skilful of the hunters crept, covered with wolfskins, among the stupid, superannuated bulls. These let the stratagem steal by them, and when at last in the south the violet column of the first smoke waved a signal above the traveling dust, the great attack began. Near at hand, the ignited shriveled grass flung up orange hands of as-

A Prairie Grove

tonished flame. And the herd caught the cruel laughter of it and the smell of man in the same instant. The straggling wolves became yelling humans, sprung up full height.

There was a buckling forward of the whole horde, driven on by flames from the rear, a wave of frantic flesh that was impacted by the return of the column's head. Between the two charges ran the naked human bodies. Through the dust and the uproar the arrows sped without a sound and stuck their taunts in flank and shoulder and chest. The bulls put down their heads and gored the earth up; they pawed defiance and glared about for the right thing to hate where everything was mounting, reddening waves of hate. But the arrows found them without an answer left to give; the knees buckled and the great forward weight unsteadily sank.

When the flames closed in, the goring began; the calves were trampled and the cows were killed by their lords. Then the herd milled in its death dance, till it had to turn and face the storm of arrows on the flank. So it rolled, a wave over its own dead, and charging blind with the blood in its eyes, broke through the Indian line and did not even see the yellow flight of its tormentors. Men fled like mice before the stampede, terror in the marrow of their

A Prairie Grove

brittle bones, and the tide of cresting hump and heaving rump hollows seethed westward, into cleaner air where the man stink and the smoke acid faded as they ran and their own snorting breath perfumed free air again.

South and north dashed the exultant flames. They too were loose now and would not stop till they had burned the prairie black and scorched the boughs of generous oak upon the farther shore of it. By their flickering light, in the gathering dusk, the men came back and began to claim their kill by the individual symbols on the arrows. There were seven hundred dead buffalo on the charred plain, and three dead men.

So they had their kill, the Illinois, and they paid their price. They took what they needed, like every tribe with hunting grounds in the range of the bison. They did not fracture the strength of the great bodily pyramid of Nature. Year after year and through the centuries the buffalo, like all the beasts of value to man, paid some toll to the cunning and the necessity of a fellow creature less strong than they. But there was no diminution in the great numbers. Save for our white men's coming, the bison would still blacken the plains, the passenger pigeons still cover the sun with the close net of their wings.

A Prairie Grove

The Indian had no real greed because, except in a small way, he knew of no markets and had nothing so movable and disturbing and universal as money. I do not say that this was more than the innocence of his ignorance. Had his numbers been like ours, he would have had to lead a different life. But no estimate of his population has ever set his numbers north of Mexico at so high a figure as ten million mouths. For the higher the block in the pyramid, the smaller it must be. If you cut away the stones at the bottom, if you pile the weight upon the top, can a pyramid stand?

For ten days there was nothing but coming and going from the village to the place of the kill. It was a ragged procession of women and dogs, slaves, catamites and old men, going out to the slaughter where it lay mountainous on the prairie. They went out empty-handed and came back laden, like a defile of ants that has found a dead thing in the woods and brings it back by infinitesimal piecemeal to the nest.

Out on the prairie the great hides came off under the knife, the mighty tongues were cut from the throats, enormous delicacy, and the steaks of the cows, always fattest at this season, were carved from the bones and tugged and staggered with back to the

A Prairie Grove

hundred fires. Around the feasting circle passed the tenderloin and fat, offered first to the old, to the visiting Osage and Mascouten and eaten in turn by the chiefs and the great warriors. The smell curled through the camp, into the bark and reed houses loose-woven for summer, suddenly chill and windy now, and the women were hungry and waited. They stole cuts and shreds of meat for the children, and kicked the leaping dogs. Out on the plain the slave captives were finishing the monstrous butchery, till the entrails and the bones were all that was left. Under night's cover the coyotes came for them.

When the steaks were jerked on the slow fires for the winter's use, and the last wild swan was pickled in brine, and the corn was dried and some of it warily buried, the tribe, like the bison, like the fowls of the air, were done with this hunting ground. They stood up and felt the cold wind at the roots of their hair, and how the sunlight on their limbs had little warmth in it. They gathered their weapons up, and mounted their medicine and their clan bundles on their hard male backs. The women took down the houses, collected and folded them; they piled the buffalo jerks and hides on the women slaves. The babies were strapped to their boards and shouldered; the children came running; even

A Prairie Grove

the poplars flung down the last of their leaves, and the fires were trodden out.

They moved from the grove by families, by groups with their dependents, the half-wild dogs running in and out between the steadily moving legs. Miles ahead already ran the stripped young scouts, but the least came last. The final figure in the deserted camp was a silent slave with three great cow jerks, two kettles, and a papoose, whose weight combined depended from the straps of buffalo skin passed round her forehead. As she straightened up from the last act of loading there was only the forest to see the sum of her burdens, great among them the curve of her pregnancy like the oblate ripeness of the pawpaw. But the tall trees were indifferent, and the squirrels bounded happily behind her back as she followed the last of the dogs into the charred prairie.

Now the rains came, and the dust was laid and the smells were washed out of the earth. Now was the season of great emptiness. A marvelous silence occupied the grove. The arriving winter birds settled their little clans without a word; they flickered through the trees like the leaves that blew off. The elk and the deer were at peace now, browsing on the last of the greenery. There was sleep in store

A Prairie Grove

for the one old he-bear that the red men had not caught; there was sleep for the woodchuck, obese as an old chief. The gophers and the chipmunks drowsed in their burrows.

Then the snow came, the white crystals spinning purely through the steely deciduous woods and falling on the bear's blowing fur to be speared or melted there. But storms overtook each other, and the snow flew as if the divinity of West were sending spirit arrow showers. So the drifts went over the head of the bear humped deep in the leaf bed with his back against the biggest fallen oak; they rose to the necks of the tallest weeds before they ceased. Then the crust was printed with the tracks of the foraging longspurs and snowflakes, and the field mice tunneled an intricate city of runways underneath the miles of prairie snow. Deep beneath the ground the muskrats worked their way toward the buried rootstocks of the water lily. More snow came, dry cold snow, and blew whispering across the glistening crust.

21

So WILDERNESS erased what had been writ in water. The coming of the Frenchmen was a false dawn, and for nearly two centuries after, history in my island grove was dark. Then, with a stumbling plod of hooves, came the day of our own people.

The progress of the oxcarts was only a mile and a half an hour, but nothing held them back.

A strange thing comes your way, wide wilderness, something you never conceived or invented, a geometrical shape, an abstraction become reality—the wheel. No Indians knew it; they only drifted slowly, like blown leaves, upon their migrations. Lumbering, bogging, lunging up, crushing, protesting, the wheels came on. For the wheel is the shape that cannot stand still. Once it was discovered, it began to roll; once it rolled, there was no stopping it.

Sounds went before the wagons, the jingle and drumming of the pots and kettles that dangled underneath the floors. There was the thick, inevitable plucking noise of the ox hooves trudging mud; sometimes the tired children cried, and sometimes a boy

A Prairie Grove

or a young wife would strum a banjo, playing *William Riley* and *Sister Phoebe*, and a man would sing, if he wasn't too tired, or a girl would sing. And always one deep strong voice or another called, "So-o—oh!" and "Gee there!" and "You, sir!" Command, backed with the laugh of the whip splashing the pool of air. Under it all the voice of ash and hickory, the squeal of the axle, the yielding of the wagon frame.

Just ahead, always just ahead, the wild pricked up its ears, flew up with a glint of rump feathers. Ohio's woods, Kentucky's woods, woods of Michigan and Indiana, fell awarely silent, and then forgot. The ruts were not deep yet. When the traveling circle of noise moved on, the birds closed up its wake with song again. The squirrels still raged, and the foxes walked along a while where the many new smells were braided, flairing sheep and chickens, dogs and leather and gun oil, and white men.

By night there was a new sight, the enormous fire. The Indians had made little fires, a few sticks, a finger of flame, a secret curl of smoke; they were always afraid that they would be seen. The white man wanted light; he wanted to see; it was as if he challenged the top of the highest maple to look down and watch him, and the wolves and bobcats to

A Prairie Grove

come to the edge of darkness and stare. They saw the big wagons with their weary shafts bowed down at their owners' feet; they saw the children running, making wavering shadows run up the trees; they saw the stubborn ox backs, the men and women who went about and stooped and rose and would not let themselves be tired. The fiddle said,

> *Oh, Sister Phoebe, how merry were we,*
> *That night we sat under the Juniper tree,*
> *The Juniper tree, heigho.*

Pioneers had to sleep at last, sunk in it, drunk with it, deep in it as animals. They did not set a guard; there was no one who could have stayed awake. They trusted in an Old Testament God, a long-bore gun, and the big, wary dogs that took everything in this wilderness to be enemy. The Indian dog was a kicked, starved, needle-fanged native jackal, more friends with the wild than with man, but having none of the wild pride. Cap and Prince and Juno and Queenie followed not from hunger so much as from faith. They had watched the old dooryard, they ran all the day now beside the wheels, and they came to the fingers that snapped for them, and nuzzled adoringly.

The night did not like them. It went away again.

A Prairie Grove

The big cat crouched in a low crotch and licked annoyance off its chops. The deer bounded off and ran a long way into the forest, but the memory of a smell grooves deep; it is there after it is gone. The fire slowly died; darkness regained the clearing; the summer stars wheeled down through the trees, and in the chill of the after-midnight hours the autumn constellations rose up, prophetic ancients. A woman's eyes would range the camp then, looking for the broad back of her husband, for the count of her children and if they were covered; in the darkness she stared at risk and struggle and stared them down. Or sometimes she missed her husband, and started up in the wagon at a crashing in the night; then he would come, his silhouette almost unrecognizable with logs and brushwood, and hearten the fire for them all. A boy, disturbed and numb, would edge away from the increeping dew and steal to the warmth of his small brother. One girl, wakeful in a family of men, would hug her own arms and hide from the firelight in her hair. Any who saw another rouse spoke low and reassuringly. These are our nights, then and still. On the immigrant ship, in the farmhouse centered in the drought waste, in the hot apartment with doors open in the thin walls, night is all body and heart.

A Prairie Grove

Day came, and the astounded woods heard the cocks crow. Cramped in their coops, ludicrous and courageous, they thrust out their necks and cried their trumpet cry. Fresh smells were flung upon the brightening air, foreign odors of bacon and coffee and wheat bread. The English speech rose clear and hard through the tree tops. The woods had heard the Shawnees talk, the Miamis, and the Potawatomis, the crows, the jays, the bellowing elk. For a little time from the days of Du Gay to the loss of New France to England, there had been some fine French speech and much bastard French of the *engagé* and the half-breed. But that language was still now, and our own was heard. Can you say that it is not beautiful? Softness is not the only beauty; grace is not better than strength. So the voices called:

"Hiram, your cattle got loose with mine, I guess."

"Susanna, this child's lost a shoe."

"Looks as if the sun would burn today."

"Find anything on your trout lines?"

"No, too many kingfishers, Nevi. I guess they got quite a catch."

These are friends, this is laughter, you wilderness. This is not clan, not *gens*, not tribe. These are Americans. They come with a joke for the worst, and take the best in silence. They pass small change of kindness freely; they call stranger brother.

"Sister, how's that boy of yours? Belly still aching?"

"Shoake, how's your wife? That rough piece back a ways yesterday must 'a' been hard on her."

"It was some hard, but it's getting along so that one thing or another's going to bring the baby soon. Not too soon it'll be, now."

"S'pose she wants a boy?"

"S'pose so. I could do with a girl this time."

"Well, remember, as long as you keep close to us, my wife's here."

"Mammy!" A child came running, calling. "Mammy, look! Can I eat them? Little apples!"

Into the cupped grubby hand the woods had given the soft, lemon-shaped May apples. But the child's father was calling to her mother, the baby fretted, crying at the breast as it lost the nipple, so the child, unnoticed, with a delicious sense of adventure, put her milk teeth into the mysterious fruit. And it was soft as custard, citric-tanged, a new taste, new food, another thing found. She ran away shouting and laughing, she did not know why. In the thickets her brothers were running the sheep back to the blaze

A Prairie Grove

and the trace; they called her to go and hunt for Belle the cow, and she went off dutifully. Suddenly under her feet a grouse covey exploded. Her heart pounded, and then she was sure again and went on. "Belle!" she called, "she, boss, boss, boss!"

22

THIS STATE began to fill up from the bottom, like a vase. At first the rivers were the highways. The Ohio and the Mississippi bore the flatboats, the keelboats, the arks, and the log rafts to the southern shores. Then the Wabash, the Vermilion, the Kaskaskia, and the Illinois let the water immigrants move inland. They came from Kentucky, Tennessee, and southern Indiana, but few of them had been born there. The black Illinois bottom lands were their third, their fourth temptation to remove. Those pioneers were born in Virginia or the Carolinas or Georgia; on the way, in the stages marked by decades, their children came forth from the race womb and were carried onward, in arms, in the wagons, the boats.

They found an enfeebled colony of French settled in the fertile hot malarial bottoms, a people whose best citizens had moved across the Mississippi into Spanish territory. Frenchmen, Indians, and Negroes dwelt together in the same ruinous houses on the tracts of treacherous richness into which the

A Prairie Grove

rivers ate with each spring flood. The dream, Du Gay, is over, and the race you planned is mongrel, without spine. It is picturesque—a sure symbol of decay—affable without power, a branch cut off. So it could only wither, and alien wheels rolled over it.

Across the sea the plump German hand of George III tried to stop the westward flood of the colonists. When the English won the Illinois country from the French, the Crown did not intend to give it to the rabble. The plan had been that it should be bestowed in time on nobles, favorites, moneylenders who could not be repaid. The King told his governors to tell those Long Rifles to come back over the mountains where they could be taxed and churched and, like feudal peasants, raise the crops an overlord most needed. This Illinois was then the western boundary of Virginia, on the maps. But there were men who without compass could line a grove across a hundred miles of unmapped prairie, who yet were unable to read a proclamation. Hopeless to send after them; those who were sent themselves remained.

When war came, George Rogers Clark with the Rangers at his back struck so swiftly that he found the royal governor Rocheblave in bed; he shook the sleeper's shoulder to inform him that all Illinois was George III's no longer.

A Prairie Grove

So he won it for these loosely united states. But even the wise, east of the Alleghenies, could be foolish. Prophesied Monroe to Jefferson:

"A great part of the territory is miserably poor especially that near Lakes Michigan and Erie, and that upon the Mississippi and the Illinois consists of extensive plains which have not had from appearances, and will not have, a single bush on them for ages. The districts therefore within which these fall will never contain a sufficient number of inhabitants to entitle them to membership in the confederacy."

In 1818 Illinois became a state. There was some padding of the census, but within ten years none would have been necessary. The vessel, slender at the bottom, was filling up. Hunters they were, a people who lived by and for the bear as the Illinois had followed the buffalo, small corn farmers coming after the hunters, southern gentry coming after these, with slaves and horses and money, turning the one-plow man out of his squatter's holdings—so they propelled each other forward in waves.

These were a forest people; they had a tradition that you had to clear the trees away before you could farm. Thus they deployed into a prairie state, avoiding the prairies, cutting down the woods. They were afraid of the prairies; these looked empty and lone-

A Prairie Grove

some. Instead of water, they held only marshes; there were rattlers and ague there and nothing over your head, nothing at your back. Men in the forested bottoms had been known to shelter a whole family, the first winter, in the hollow of a giant sycamore—such trees were in America in those days. But it was not in the experience of the southerner to make a sod hut; his children could find the cattle in the woods, but it seemed that on the prairies, where there was no timber for the snake rail fence, the beasts might wander over the world's rim.

Slowly the farms and houses crept northward, up the bottoms, meeting the Kickapoo and Mascoutens, the Sacs and Foxes. But the Black Hawk War, descending on the center of the state like the whirling tip of a tornado, caught the northern settlements up in fire and death. Even when the old chief looked back defeated from the Iowa shore and said, *"It is a beautiful land; I give it to you; enjoy it,"* the scare had not died on the frontier. The southern man, the brown rifle tall as a tall boy, the black slave and his muscle, the Lincoln type, the traditional pioneer, were not destined to reach my island grove. So it missed many familiar and storied things.

We love those things with a wry smile for them—the literal Gospel, the grown women going about

A Prairie Grove

their duties on bare feet over the earthen floor, the house and all the many implements hewn out of the continent's toughest timbers with a ringing simple art. The loom was not here, nor the traditional pattern. Neither was the old ballad from the southern highlands, nor the crackling joke, the fried cooking, the yellow complexion, the lordly male idleness, the feckless spawning, the ragged dooryard deep in weathered chips, the 'possum feasts, the whiskey jug.

To the north a different culture was coming, that of my own people. But it was dammed back longer; it was held away by the lack of roads and great rivers, and by the Indian reservations. When it came, in the eighteen-twenties, with a rattling of slow wheels at first, and then by the Great Lakes and the new canals, it was no random movement propelled by the palm of inscrutable forces. Men from New England and New York and Pennsylvania came for business, for opportunity, for deep soil and breadth of view. They talked about manifest destiny as they came; they saw empire shining; they balanced the pro-slavery elements of the southern counties with their consciences and their votes. It was commercial vision and it was industrial civilization that armed them; their backs were strong and straight not so much through bodily endurance as by belief that God re-

A Prairie Grove

veals His will to everyone directly and so no one who has enough examined himself need falter.

If you like them, these people, more than the southern pioneers, or if you like them less, you cannot say that one way, one dream, one countenance, was more American than the other. Only my people's way, my ancestors', that of the settlers in my grove, is the unsung. They have somehow not found their way into romance and sentiment, for they are not a vanished people, or a defeated people, or anachronistic. They could drive a nail with one true blow; they built a strong house. They planted, they did not cut down; they made the straight roads. In the Civil War, under incompetent generals, without a military tradition, with nothing hotter than principle to uphold them, they kept their ranks in defeat and took victory as the end of terrible business.

There are many people it is easier to admire; chivalry, the samurai tradition, grace in the art of living, the glamour of lost causes—these are properties, stock scenery, of the dramatists and the romantics. But these others, these plain pacific Midwesterners, were the sort who got a school up as soon as the home chimneys were smoking. They filled the sink holes in, and they planted lilacs in a straight row from

A Prairie Grove

the door to the gate. When they left New England they took its new tolerances with them.

There were wholesome indications that New England's granite faith in its soul's rightness was cracking and weathering. New Englanders were beginning to travel, to learn modern languages, to shift from farming, fishing, and shipping toward industry, and so doubts and doctrines blew over them. As the maritime empire receded from the east, New Englanders turned west, filled with a zeal that was sublimated religiosity. Men who had seen Canton, Penang, Sunda, Bombay, Nagasaki, and Russia sent their sons west into the ocean of land. Asa Goodner was rolling west with his family and his little apple seedlings, looking for a home site, where the raising of a log house would not be done to enhance the dignity of labor, where loneliness would be only half a privilege, and the celibate life no use to man or woman.

23

Asa Goodner's father, Amoy, seems to have been the first come-outer in the family. He was born in China because his mother insisted on making the voyage out on the *Hope of Salvation*, Salem Goodner, Master. That was his first offense, and his second was that he took no interest in returning to the land of his birth, either for gain, curiosity, or for the mere satisfaction of his uncles and brothers. The Goodner family had always followed the sea, that is to say, they had always followed it in the brief history of America. In tracing them back to the south of England, I find that a great many of them were shepherds, sextons, potters, curates, and tenant farmers. But an American family will admit to hangings in its history before it will confess peasant origins, so Goodners, of course, have always followed the sea.

On the rocky cape between Marblehead and Salem, Amoy had the insolence to build a house that turned its back to the virile ocean, and there to breed sheep. Yes, sheep, of all maggoty cattle! New Eng-

A Prairie Grove

land is used to religious independence of mind, but Amoy's come-outing was not at the dictation of his conscience. It was not even a new commercial venture, but an abstract curiosity about ovine genetics. Not, of course, that he or anyone else employed such language. They said, "Goshen, Amoy, there's no future in that!"

When Amoy had had enough of this, he drove his flocks over the Berkshires to Herkimer County in New York, and gave his family the final shock by marrying the daughter of a music master of Troy. Her name was Catherine O'Brien, and she sang too much about the house to be quite seemly. You have to know about this Irish girl before you understand the next generation. She put the warmth in their hearts; she accounts for the dark strain in about half the children, and she was prophetic because she represents that racial admixture in which America came to take pride. She added the touch of the histrionic to the taciturn Goodner strain; she gave it the only musical ear that it had ever had since the first Goodner was able to flat a tone and a half while singing a hymn next to the bellow of an organ. To a line threatened with extinction through miscarriages, one-child sterility, and a morbid chastity, she brought wholehearted fecundity. She had twins three times,

A Prairie Grove

and twice as many girls as boys. In short, she did everything possible to break up the Goodner traditions, multiply its descendants while erasing its name, and strengthen the stock while altering it.

Amoy adored her; he did not miss a detail of what she was doing to the sainted Goodner family. He saw in place of the steel-blue Goodner eyes and the thin commanding lips the laughter in his children's faces and the look of passion that flowered early on their mouths. He went on quietly improving the stock of his sheep, importing the first Merinos ever seen in New York; he took sheep, wife, daughters, and sons to Cattaraugus County and went to raising grapes as well. Catherine is buried there. Without coercion, he managed to marry his girls off to the men that looked right to his eye. He was not mistaken in his genetic instincts; they live there still, the many descendants of those daughters. Two sons, I find, were killed at Lundy's Lane; two I cannot trace; Asa, the youngest, came west in Andrew Jackson's Administration, with his wife, whom he always addressed by her full maiden name of Mary Tramble, his nine children, and Amoy, his father, still coming-out.

For his part, Asa had had enough of sheep. He was interested in apples; he wanted to plant. Good

A Prairie Grove

stock was, to his reason also, a first principle. He had the Goodner missionary zeal, but it took its own form. He wanted to plant the prairie to fine trees; to stand under such was to stand in grace. He had studied medicine in Buffalo, but he did not want to use the lancet; he wanted to graft the delicate upon the strong. That was why, perhaps, he had chosen Mary Tramble. She seemed to him, after her twelfth child—three died in infancy—still a flower upon a fragile stem. He adored children; he thought of the instruction of them as a kind of planting, and delighted in it. He believed that girls should learn the sciences; he thought you should be seasoned with forty-five winters before the Bible was good for you, and no one before in the family had ever thought it worth while to learn a foreign language. So, in his way, came-out tall Asa, so tall his shoulders were never quite straight, bent a little in his smiling attention to the slighter about him.

They came in two wagons; one was a big Conestoga built on the schooner lines with a boat-shaped bottom, hind wheels double the size of the forward, topped with a weathered housing of tow linen and drawn by four big horses pulling in a gigantic harness, its iron trace chains jangling. The other was a low boxed wagon drawn by a lightly harnessed pair

A Prairie Grove

of mules; Amasa, the oldest boy, drove it, swaying with easy unconscious rhythm to every jolt.

If Amasa was then as serious as he turns up later in the family annals, he never wasted a smile for anything which was not obviously funny, upon this travel; he drove on steadily and kept the smaller of his brothers and sisters behind him in order. He was supposed to look after the twins Nancy and John Paul, fertile in monkey-fingered diversions, Sybil, a throwback to Catherine O'Brien, so dark as to be almost a case of melanism, dramatic and disobedient, and Timothy, who was fifteen, quiet, observant, with gentle hands that learned about everything they touched.

In the big Conestoga, with the trunks, chests of drawers, and the bedstead in which Catherine had borne her children and died, rode Mary Tramble, her eldest daughter Patience, Rhoda, who was nineteen, and Amoy, meditative on a trunk, nursing a cane. Rhoda liked to sit beside her father, looking forward; she could watch the road come on forever with a zest that life's repetitions could not abate. Patience sat in the back and looked after the scenes and the days and the desires that went glimmering into the vanishing point. They say, in the family, that she cried all the way; the others pretended not

A Prairie Grove

to see it. They never knew for whom she cried; the girl had a tight mouth; privacy with her was religious. Their fears for her hovered between the possibility of a decline and old maidenhood. Ahead, on the white stallion Washington, rode Franklin who had all the good looks for the boys of the family, and behind him, postilion, young Delia the romantic, who loved her brother with a purely temporary intensity pending, though she did not know it, the first possible transfer.

When they drew up for the night, in Ohio, when they stopped at a well in Indiana to ask for water, when Asa gave apple stock to settlers for whose orchards he had a contemptuous pity, when Delia, without speaking, could draw men and boys to her, or Timothy for the first time in his life showed fight, at cruelty to an animal, broke a boy's tooth, and begged pardon for that—strangers, looking the Goodners over, recognized a clan, and a clan way. The family trailed the memory of themselves, and, long after, people talked about those Goodners, them Goodners, those strangers, the man with the apples, the girl with the eyes and her quiet sisters. They had a way with them that sure was good-natured; they had mighty fine horses; those apples were bet-

A Prairie Grove

ter'n even he said. A pity they didn't stay—folks you'd like to know.

The strongest bond of this clan was its loose articulation. All its members had a tolerance for its various differences. It did not cohere under the compulsion of aristocratic traditions, peasant penury, religion, thrashings, or sentimentality. To plant, to grow, to come-out, to fling the seed wide and take responsibility for what you planted—they lived this way so openly that they never called it a creed or held it up as sacred.

I can tell this much about them because I know them. Their way of life persists, and by this present I can tell them. I do not think of them as unique; I meet Goodners in many houses, and on the street I look in their children's happy eyes. Sometimes I think of them when a railway conductor accepts my invitation to talk, or when an old lady, enjoying her son's wealth, remembers the early hard times for me. Say, if you like, that the paternalistic peasant family is more cohesive, or there is glamour in a line whose admiral ancestors painted by Romney and Holbein look down from the walls; the Goodners are our way. Theirs are the five-sixths of the American marriages that do not break up in divorce; they are the people who combine fidelity with freedom. Not unique, not

A Prairie Grove

picturesque—unless by grace of time past—and not wholly enlightened, but aware of that. There is no formula for Goodners, and you cannot make a class or theory out of them; their individualism is a total barrier toward regimenting them.

I wonder if they did not grow that six-foot individualism of theirs in the old abundance. And their tolerance in the breadth of the prairie view. It was not tolerance that accepted for itself, or does today accept, every point of view. It is part of the knot twist in their mental timber that they are refractory to a great deal of bosh and even more to decadence. They turn the edge of many blades. They are steadfast, but they grow, yet not so that you can predict them. Because they are free, you never know what they will accept next.

These are the people who fought a war for the privilege of being united to brothers who did not wish to stay with them; they believed in a war that would end wars and make their way safe; some think they are mighty fools. Many of these thinkers now wish the Goodners to believe in class intolerance or race intolerance; perhaps they can be fooled again. But when they are, you will never get the requisite hate out of them, and you will not be able to prevent

A Prairie Grove

them from admitting it when they have been wrong and laughing deeper than their critics. That makes them an infrangible people, still living by the manitou they found in the sky when the wagon wheels rolled them west.

24

AND ALL THE TIME, while the state filled up from the bottom, when the soldiers and women were killed at Fort Dearborn in 1812, the island grove was there, tall and lordly. But in the changing weather of history, it had drifted far away again; it was remote, sighted sometimes by a *voyageur*, a commissioner of Indian business or a party of Miamis or Mascoutens. The Illinois had gone, for in a luckless hour one of their band had murdered Tecumseh, and the Shawnees in their rage had sworn to wipe them from the earth. They kept their vow, and the affable, treacherous, libidinous people whom Prud'homme had tried so hard to love had been blown like smoke and ashes, driven like their buffalo, west over the prairie till the last beaten remnants were homeless beggars among the settlers of the Spanish bottoms and the tribes that once they had enslaved.

After them you have the Mascoutens. They were prairie Potawatomis; they had horses, and gorgeous beadwork on their leggings, robes, and moccasin flaps. The Jesuit fathers who knew them said that

A Prairie Grove

their women were noted for chastity and the men, not so well-shaped as the soft Miamis, were taller and more rugged. They had more ceremony and less bestiality than their predecessors; they were braver, and they had no luck in European politics.

They sided with the French against the English, and with the English against the Americans, and under the spell of Tecumseh's enlightenment they had done away with their old gods only to find that the new were not invincible. They sold land recklessly at first; presently they saw that the more of the white man's money they took, the more they were become paupers and dependents. Once they had learned to need their luxuries, there was no resource or wealth in all their country that could pay for them. They had broken faith with Nature; they had stepped out of the pattern of the aboriginal fauna and had got into the deadly treadmill of the peoples whom white men call natives. This is to say that they exploited their inheritance, and the white men bought it under the name of raw materials. They gave back manufactured articles to the Mascoutens, and in this sort of deal one side must take a loss.

Hundreds of miles beyond the frontier, the Indians felt the deep disturbance. It is almost forgotten now, but there were many settlers who paid the Indians

A Prairie Grove

to hunt for them, to bring them daily meat. The first settlements subsisted, in part, by tapping the resource of regions far beyond the horizon. Trade, like a new river, cut across Indian life; it disturbed the whole lay of their land; it flowed away and never came back. Pride and independence and stamina and some deep prehistoric rhythm were washed away by it. So that there was nothing that an Indian would not beg for; the Indian girl became the prostitute of the frontier; then smallpox came. One legend has it that an Indian stole the blanket from under a man left dying with it; that is probably only a frontier joke, of the "serve 'em right" variety.

There is no record of the whole Indian tragedy, only scattered references, sad words of chiefs: *We burned our tents and houses; we were afraid to touch the dead, and dragged them away with a hooked stick under the chin; why will you not give us whiskey now? You gave it when you wanted our land; now if we had it we could forget what once we owned. We do not know what to think of you; your children never get enough land. We have listened to you until our land is nearly gone. Our footsteps have passed off it.*

I am not certain that the Mascoutens ever had a village here in my grove. They used it still for a

A Prairie Grove

portage, but they went where the white men went, like dogs at the back doors.

And a great commercial destiny had missed the grove. When the Chicago portage was discovered to be superior, trade went that way. If it had not, I should have the Union Stockyards here; this spot would hold in its hand the fifty reins of the greatest railway plexus in the world; the lumber trade and the grain trade of the continent would lie heavy here; there would be the ringing of the steel mills and the hell glow of them on the night sky. I should have three million neighbors, most of them Italians, Swedes, Poles, Jews, Germans, Hungarians, Czechs, and Negroes. I am not feeling superior in my loneliness; I like Italians, Czechs, Germans, and so on; I like to wade through the shoals of their children in Maxwell Street; I like to look upon their window gardens from the Elevated. I have never yet read the story of Chicago as I would like to read it, the rise of the brownstone front, the waves beating around Hull House, the detonation of the Haymarket riots, the manifest dream of beauty in the first World's Fair, the big men who shouldered the city up. But that is not this story.

For greatness missed you, my oaks and my prairie; so you are still here, and the sweet slough chains

A Prairie Grove

are not drained; they touch fingers in April and May. So the depths are here, the green perspectives, the blue shadows, the hard tang of the goldenrod and the complaint of the wheeling hawks. I hear the lisp and the hum of the summer afternoon; I see the light lie on every leaf. You are forgotten again, and there are only the memories of good endeavor here.

I cannot find a certain mention of this grove between 1673 and the Goodners' coming. In all that time it had no English name; it drops off the maps, it disappears from travelers' tales. Sometimes I think I find it, but never so that I can identify it as an historian would demand. A doctor says:

"I was taken by the Indians a long way, up a river which I now believe may have been the Kilimick, and arrived after dark at an encampment in a thick growth of trees. The patient, a very old Indian woman, had died before I arrived. I was treated with every courtesy and feasted upon pigeon and bear, which tastes like sweet pork, and some sort of a root which they dig out of the marshes. In the morning I was paid in beaver skins, and departed as I came. I remember that it seemed to me I had never beheld such splendid oaks; many of them had boughs which swept the ground. There were thick cables of grapevine festooning the woods, and the women were gathering an incredible harvest of hickory nuts."

A Prairie Grove

The two Hawley girls were captured in what was then part of the immense county of Crawford, in the War of 1812. They were made to walk or run a hundred and twenty miles in four days, and arrived, according to the memoir of Elizabeth, at a grove near a river toward noon of the fifth day. They were greeted by a band of women who at once began to beat them with sticks, out of revenge for their dead sons and husbands. After a week of bullying, they were finally adopted as slaves. They discovered that as soon as they were willing to live and behave like Indian girls, they were better treated. Nevertheless, one of them died of starvation, and the other was saved from the same fate by going to the blanket of a chief. The whole band removed westward after a few months, and when ten years later Elizabeth was restored to her race at St. Louis, she had forgotten what the Indians called the grove and the river. She remembers the multitude of the ducks, and the elk fawn that she found in the woods, that played dead, lying limp and still in her arms but with its bright eyes still open and sparkling; she remembers how she and her sister tried to live by eating blackberries and bitter acorns, and how she had to cut the marsh reeds for the mat she took to her master.

This is all, and it is nothing. I have looked con-

A Prairie Grove

scientiously, but I am not fully sorry that I cannot fix my island grove in that span of time that was so long and so indifferently meager of human event in the wilderness. I like the thought of it, lost for long intervals, left on one side, adrift, becalmed, self-contained. The trees I walk under, the tallest ones, were young then; they did most of their growing through those years. They would not be here had they been found too soon.

Asa Goodner says the grove was empty when he came. He liked it so. At the land office he bought a section, half prairie and half grove, from the government. It would do for a beginning. He knew how clean the slate was, and he liked it so. He got his apples in before the fall rains came, while the family was still sleeping in the wagons. He started out with many kinds, Greenings and Bellflowers, Rambos and Russets and Red Vandevers. The rains came, the roots struck; they were sucking life before the frost. And he thought of the orchards that his grandchildren would know, and how their teeth would bite through the deep red coats of the Vandevers, and how hardy the Russets were, and of the beautiful shape of the Bellflowers. But he loved the Rambos best, for their perfume and their sweetness and their clean white flesh.

25

The Goodners found the grove in August, the last of August, the season that I call green autumn. That means the goldenrod is tall, the asters are in flower, and the woodbine is turning color. But the oaks are green, and green are the mossy-fringed burr cups; the haws upon the thorn tree are not yet red. The world at that moment has all the depth and bounty of summer. But a high cool wash goes through the treetops and they clamor gently at coming event.

The black ground mists of heat are lifted and blown to Jericho, and across the prairie the depths and the groves and the winding river woods rush nearer at a stride. Yesterday you could not see the shape of Alison's barns; now you can distinguish each pigeon's wing in the swirling flash around the silo. Now is the moment when you can find the first secretive bluebottle gentian; the jays and the crows talk as though it were already October. It is that part of autumn that is thoughtful without decay, lusty without being carnal. There is nothing to regret as yet, and all you intend to do still seems possible.

A Prairie Grove

In the old days this was the season when the travelers fell in love with Illinois. The swamp chains were dry then, the prairie was not blackened with October fires, and you would not believe then, with the weather exultant and optimum, in the cruelty of winter. The game was jumping; jacksnipe came back from the north; the sandpipers clinked and ran around the last moist border of the sloughs; mud was infrequent now and good. Mud of the marvelous old black woman, earth, irrepressibly fertile, clothed in the lisping sedges where the big game birds walked, scuttled chickenwise, rose up unwillingly and, unwary, took the time to wheel and gave the marksman his moment. There seemed still to be endless plenty, though the buffalo were gone; the elk were gone, and so were the cougar, fisher, gray fox, marten, beaver, and otter.

No one knows just when or why they went; there was more concerted attack upon deer and wolves, yet these stayed longer. The others shrank away; they lost together curiosity and courage; the gun and the dog, the fence and the plow, were too much for them, and they met something even steelier. Call it intolerance or mastery, we all have it, and so possess it utterly that we scarcely feel aware of it. White man—and it is just as true of white woman—momently demands that all things should kneel and

A Prairie Grove

bare their necks; then we decide what we shall spare. The creatures that are not either useful or humble draw back onto their haunches and snarl and stare; they have the military privilege of dying like braves, but they may not live.

The fragments of memoirs, the letters, the county histories, the old women with folded hands remembering what their grandmothers said, do not tell me everything I know. From them I get only phrases: They turned the teams loose, and the horses were so wild for the pea vines that you could hardly find them or drive them in at night. John Paul and Nancy began to fill Nancy's skirt with hickory nuts until they saw that there were so many that you would not have to gather them up until you needed them. Asa called, "Mary Tramble, come and see this oak opening; do you think you'd like the house here?" So that's how it came to be built here, you see.

That is the way the family story goes. But I know the rest; I know the grove and the weather, I know Sybil from her pictures and Timothy from his fame and Asa from his apple trees, bent over now with great bearings and storms and this wry miracle of living.

Sybil walked about alone, having decided that this would be a good place and moment in which to try

A Prairie Grove

out luxurious unhappiness. She was eleven, and in the dusk she carried about with her she lived a separate life. She did not regard her present situation as romantic; her family had simply chosen to move far out into loneliness. They had swept her to an island as well removed from the ship lanes of glory as one could imagine, and rescue seemed almost impossible. Yet she sent up, hopelessly but faithful to herself, the thin signal of her moods. Through the woods rang the song of the ax, and the white chips flew over the wild lawns.

Asa and Amasa and Franklin could all master a log; Asa says he was considered the best ax man and general ranger in Cattaraugus County, and the dovetailed logs are still here to speak for him. Nothing he did ever warped. Amasa was interested in the engineering problem of the upper walls and the roof; he loved the theory of a thing, but in the practical Yankee way. He was not curious about the impossible; he simply liked to do the work first in his head; he liked laws, premises that you could hang your weight on.

Franklin worked because it got you where you wanted; secretly he did not hope or believe that he was going to remain here. He wanted money, and he saw that money could be made to work for you

A Prairie Grove

and could make others work for you. Imagine waiting for apple trees to grow up, waiting on weather for your harvest! He was patient now, with the iron discipline of those who know what and how much they want and how far away from it they are. The house he saw in his mind, the mirrors, the carpets, the table, the bedroom, the woman—they were already realities to him, and already torments. For it makes the unimaginative suffer to imagine.

The twins came and begged for tasks to do; they put chips in a basket, and Patience began to weave her one spell. She could cook a hickory limb, so the family always says, so you could enjoy eating it, and she set the cookstove up under the trees. In spite of meager materials, she found something to keep her hand in all day, and this kept the twins trotting and stooping for wood, until they learned to hide from her.

Rhoda and Delia were as busy as their brothers; they were dutiful and gay. But each was busied in her head with her own desires. Delia had a face like the morning; you would not have supposed that spite, envy, or untruth could find an instant's lodging behind such a countenance. Her body was a song; she could not move except seductively. She was not, however, so eager to love as to be loved, or rather—though she did not know it—to be desired. Rhoda

A Prairie Grove

was the quiet one. She was not girlish; at nineteen she was a young woman, with purpose and control in her movements; she was more awake to love than her sisters and thought less about it. She had such health that only to live was rapture, and she wanted to give herself away, health and rapture and purpose all together. How she might do this she understood very well. No one had awakened her; she just woke quietly to find the light come.

Woman came to northern Illinois from the northeastern states just as she had been back home. She was not the barefooted serf of the squirrel hunters; dressed in preposterous modesty, dragging her heavy skirts over unshorn turf, yet her eyes were not on the ground but looked levelly in the face of future. What she intended would make more changes than the French priests' faith. Even then, of course, there were kinds of women without number. Some the wilderness killed, as Delia was to die at twenty across the Missouri. To some, whom Eastern life would have stifled, it gave air to breathe. It gave a field to girls like Patience, endowed with the missionary spirit. To the artist it offered only thistles. But Rhoda was of that breed of girls that hardship strengthens but does not coarsen, that childbirth does not kill,

A Prairie Grove

that heartbreak does not conquer. Some must have been your mothers, and some, your daughters, will carry your immortality in their hands.

It is easy now to look back and choose, out of the great Goodner sisterhood, Rhoda to stand for the tree that would thrust root and bear fruit. But in a place that lacks them, all women make you think of the same things. And Mary Tramble's daughters, moving roofless still under the trees, their skirts whipped by an aborigine wind, were indistinguishably promising, awaiting what the frontier and its man would make of them.

On the day when the bottom logs were just going into place, Chance Randelman rode into the opening on his roan and offered his help to Asa.

Mary Tramble did not approve of him and seems to have said so. He instantly magnetized all the girls except Nancy. But he paid his court to their mother. I see in her picture the straightness of her back, the touch of fashion in her very small waist, a little of the belle still in her grandmother face. She has grass-flower-blue eyes, and they make her look more helpless than she was; her very small wrists were quite strong, and the whole family was a little vain of the tininess of her foot. This sort of woman, however

A Prairie Grove

busy her life, makes a life study of man, and she knows a dangerous one when he comes her way.

He swung from his horse like a condescension, but he knew the arts of the frontier. He took command without waiting to be invited. He had practiced rule of thumb for Amasa's painstaking theory, and he put the heart into the log-raising that Franklin could not feel. At the noon halt he rode away with a bow and a flourish, and came back in an hour with Jean Kiercereau, a half-breed who cut lifting poles out of ash saplings at two ax blows apiece; then he trimmed the branches off at the top till he had a crotch. With three of these poles you could work a log up to the top of the walls.

When it came to the roof, old Amoy knew what he was doing better than anyone else. Then the children were set to making clay cats out of slough earth and wisps of wild hay; the twins splashed the mud and laughed; Timothy dreamed as he did it; Sybil pretended she was a slave and forced to it. So they made the chinking for the stick chimney and filled the spaces between the logs; then a decent whitewash coat lightened the interior. Amoy laid the first hearthfire that smoked up the damp chimney. The family clustered around to watch it struggle and catch and glow.

A Prairie Grove

Against the door frame Chance Randelman leaned, scornful of the way the fire was built, the vanity of the cookstove, the bright walls, and so much domestic ceremony. Secretly he was resenting the intrusion; he had killed a fawn on this spot, and the doe. He shot the fawn first, knowing that the doe would come back to it, and of course she did, and he shot her. He could imitate the bleating of a fawn, the jittering of a squirrel, or the blowing of a turkey cock. He had that rare, inhuman ability to call wild ducks to him. He knew just how to take hold of animal instincts; then he pulled his quarry to him, and killed it clean. He loved what he killed, and was never satisfied.

That first night Patience outdid herself. Kiercereau contributed the corn; Chance brought the saddle of venison and insisted on roasting it himself, out of doors, larding it with bacon fat. They ate under the blessing of down-sweeping boughs where the cool dusk gathered; they were tired but they had a sense of ceremony. Everyone understood the significance of a roof in place and a smoke wisp rising through the treetops.

Kiercereau was as sensitive to this as the others; he was bewildered, illiterate, a little dark musky man whose clearest thoughts were only groping, but

A Prairie Grove

animal-neat in his motions. He looked these strangers over, and he wondered why Randelman put himself to any trouble for them; it could only be because there were women here. The hunter was now paying attention to Sybil, but this was a hunter's blind. Yet how the little decoy liked it!

Thin curtains of darkness dropped soundlessly between the farther trees, moving as conclusive music. The embers sputtered with the last fat drippings.

Kiercereau thought frankly about the three older girls but looked respectfully. For himself, he would have chosen the cook; no man leaves a woman who is a good cook. He thought the middle girl would be a strong worker; the youngest, the one with the eyes, was the kind of woman who would want things, an expensive wife. Not that anyone had ever heard of Randelman's going wife-hunting; he had women where he wanted them. And what a fool a woman was to look at a man's face!

There was no event that night. Significant moment, it was not part of a story. To make a story the teller must select out what will forward a plot, and cast aside the quiet matrix that holds incident together. I like what the storyteller throws away. I like to think about the scraping good-by of the half-breed, the shock of the ground under the roan's departing

A Prairie Grove

hooves, the family that came in out of moonshine and dewfall to find the embers on their hearth. I like old Amoy's stick put to stand by the door while he slept, and the clean smell of the wood in the new roof, the harping singsong of green autumn insects. And the bulk, the shape, the fact, significant and blunt, of the house in the midnight clearing.

26

THE RAINS CAME. In a tropical land you can tell almost to a day when they will begin; in Illinois we do not even know whether we will get any, and when they start we do not know when they will stop. In autumn they bring the feel of winter; they drive in long veils through the trees and they walk on the face of the grasslands. That year they filled the prairie hollows; they brought the swamps back, and they watered Asa's apple roots newly struck in the ground.

On the roof they beat in gusts. They clattered fit to empty the sky, but it was never emptied. They would finger the roof for hours, like the tattoo of an idle girl's nails upon a table; then the downpour would commence again, until you could hear the whistle of the drops through the air. Old Amoy's roof was tight; his seed beneath it quietly exulted in it. There was a faint violet curtain of smoke that clung just under the boards, beginning to stain them; the smell of it was in the women's hair; the men and the boys had bits of log bark like snuff about

A Prairie Grove

their coats. The fire was fed daylong and never went out at night. There was wood enough to feed it, all the deep woods behind the house full of the dead trees that had never been cleared away, full of the flung-down branches and twigs; the men had their axes and their arms; they were part of the vital current, so racial and immemorial, that flows from the sun to the earth, the earth to the trees, the trees to flame again.

So they lived with the four elements. The ancients thought that fire and air were male, earth and water were woman stuff. The Goodners were moderns; they were not mystical; they had the Yankee knack for hitching things together. They believed not in what the elements might do to them, but in what presently they could do with the elements. They blessed fertile rain and spear-armed fire without having to kneel or propitiate; their rites were practical and unconscious.

The rain fell and fell, and the family hugged its unity and went forward with its living. Timothy taught Sybil, and Patience taught the twins, and Asa taught Delia and Timothy. Amasa knocked up shelves; he ran a shelf all the way around the big room and made them grow up like bracket fungi on each side of the doors. In the doorway, with

A Prairie Grove

the smoke curling faintly out behind him and the rainy air drinking into the room around his shoulders, he looked out across the veiled landscape and saw the unused, refractory land. He thought of wheat, the intense golden freight of its heads, the tawny sheet of its stubble and the wealthy run and lisp of the grain pouring into the bins.

Delia sewed; she began to take a sudden pleasure in dressing the child Sybil who had a smoldering hunger for clothes. Rhoda kept the house clean; the broom handle had a soft shine upon it that her hands gave it, but she did not notice it; in her mind, awake and frank, she thought about Chance Randelman. At the little desk that had come all the way from Salem, Asa plotted grafts and plantings. Moving about the house, Mary Tramble created that subtle order and grace that makes a lady's home, however crude. At night she would sit writing by candlelight to all her kin in Buffalo; she wrote across the lines too, which is what makes it so difficult for me to read her record of those days and nights.

Then suddenly, in October, the sky cleared. Amoy didn't know how he knew it, but he promised that the deluge was over, and he was right. The woods were drenching still for two days; then under wind and sun they were dry and summery again. But it was Indian summer, and in the woods was heard the rejoicing chorus of the cricket frogs, hopping pilgrims on their way back to the renewed marshes. The ground was populous with them for some days; then the squirrels began to leave. They streaked through the trees as if something were after them; they were so numerous that they lost their charm and became as deserting rats. They went south as if they felt cold weather coming, but it was not true migration, for those that went never came back. It was dispersal from overpopulous centers. The squirrels seldom now behave this way, but the old huntters remember it, Audubon wrote of it, and in the annals of this grove the great squirrel drive of that autumn brought back Chance Randelman. He took Timothy out to teach him how to shoot; he gave Sybil all the pelts her arms could hold, and she buried her dark little face in them luxuriously.

Then the squirrels were gone, and Chance was off to Elk Grove for turkey. The last flowers flecked the woods, goldenrod went to tawny down, the aster bracts were empty and silver, and mysteriously bloomed gall-of-the-earth, nodding, long and withdrawn of flower, above its lion's-foot leaves. Dawn and evening were wintry; the noons were soft, gold

A Prairie Grove

in the core, blue on the far edges; sounds came from a long distance clearly in a deepening silence. Earth sighed its warmth away, a little more each day, but there was still heat in the midday sun. Air smelled of far-off fires and leaf mold breaking under the footfall. It had such ache and beckon in it, this Indian summer, that it drew them all outdoors. It promised, but it did not say what.

Timothy set muskrat traps by the river; Franklin got on his horse and rode to Chicago for candles and salt and powder and flitches. Rhoda felt her first impulse to avoid her brothers and sisters; she had to walk; she felt a longing for neighbors; she swept the horizon for smoke, listened in the woods for hoofbeats.

Each day no one came, and each day it seemed that this was very certainly the last when the bluejay would ripple his come-hither call and the ants would have the strength to toil on the high cones tall as her knees. She was looking west over the prairie when Randelman rode up behind her back. He swung off when he was abreast of her, dropping close to her side, bringing the smell of leather and gun oil and game. There were seven bobwhite slung to the saddle; the wind still made their feath-

A Prairie Grove

ers alive, but their eyes were dead, and the odor and feel of kill stole out from them.

She was quiet and did not look at him much, so that he could not understand her. A girl walking alone in the wind on the edge of woods perplexed him; he had thought at first that she was waiting and looking for him. But she was too natural for a girl in love; he seemed to have interrupted some dream of hers with his presence.

And it began to interest him to imagine what it would take to wake her. He had not thought her the most attractive of the sisters, but he looked now at her arms, three-quarters bare, and it came to him that he was tired of taking and wanted to be given love. The pattern of the promise, the bride, the suckled baby, the mutual labor, sprang up out of this hour like a swift flower with exciting fragrance. For the first time he did not know what he could do with a woman, or how he could come at her heart. The thought that he might kiss her made his heart turn once with hurt in it, like that of a boy who has never tried what he is plotting for the next instant.

The roan mare watched what her master did with a mellow eye; she knew women from men very well; she could sense fright in a human being electrically,

A Prairie Grove

but after a moment she saw the woman grow quiet. The mare cropped the sweet deep grass with a seeking muzzle; at the bottom of the warmth, weather-wise she sensed the coming frost.

It came, under crystal stars in a black sky, Fomalhaut peering one-eyed and autumnal over the southern rim of the world. In the house the fires spit at the coals; the winds sang at the chinks; Rhoda was silent with her first secret from those who loved her. In the mirror Delia did and undid, never satisfied, the tingling wide web of her hair.

27

Franklin came back from Chicago with ideas. The town was a mudhole, and full of riffraff, but there was money in it. It had a future, perhaps not as great as that of St. Louis, but shrewd men saw it already. Franklin, though he had the least interesting mind in the family, was witness, through a long life, of the city's giant growth; the family to this day remembers scraps of his tales about its beginnings. And I am remembering for them the night when Franklin got home, a changed son and brother, his pockets and heart stuffed with secrets, some of which he told them.

He prepared them first by wonder tales of Chicago. Besides the officers at the fort, some of them with families, the town was aswarm with peddlers and grog sellers and sharpers. At the mere rumor of a canal from Lake Michigan to the Illinois, land fever had infected the whole place, and men in its delirium were buying lots for which they would never have to pay because they would sell them tomorrow at a profit.

A Prairie Grove

Everybody was pursuing claims. There were claims on the government and claims against the Indians. The Indian agents were charged with cheating their wards, and everybody was frantic to get into the Indian agents' boots. The bounty on wolves had resulted in the importation of wolf hides from Canada; at the same time there were men who were trying to get the government to pay them for the pigs that the wolves had eaten, so they did not want the wolves killed at all.

Franklin had seen New York financiers there, their gray beaver hats stuffed full of promissory notes, mortgages and summonses. There were hunters from beyond the Missouri, in their skins and beards like Robinson Crusoe's; there were horse dealers and horse stealers, nearly identical professions, Franklin opined. In the mud, in the smells of pigs and horses, in the rank, fresh-water odor of the lake, much trade and more opportunity were abroad. There were profit taking and cheating going on all day without apparently the compensatory action of natural or moral laws; a big profit did not mean that someone else had to take a loss, and transgression of the commandments was not punished, in this place without a God. At night the people who tried to sleep in the handful of crowded log houses,

A Prairie Grove

in the fort, in the wagons, even on the beach, were kept awake by the dismal celebrations of the Indians; they howled and sang and powwowed over their liquor in worse than savagery.

Now Franklin brought out his first secret and proposal. He was a young man of initiative. Unused money was a crime, in his view of it, and like all moralists, he was ready to take on other people's welfare. So he had taken seventy-five dollars of the family cash, to buy an option on five acres at the mouth of the Chicago river. I can hear the family conference on Franklin's astounding coup. His transgression of their moral law was so obvious that they did not need to point it out to him, and at first they were dumb with astonishment, for they had their first revelation of Franklin's own come-outance. They were unacquainted with the morality of the banker, which is, except as hemmed in by law, to seize every opportunity at the lowest price, use others' money for their own good, and then honestly pay them their share of the profits.

Old Amoy's voice: "What's the land good for, Franklin?"

Asa speaking: "Must be pretty swampy, right at the mouth of the river."

A Prairie Grove

Franklin's mother: "Is it the sort of place we could take the girls, my son?"

Amasa protested: "Seems to me we've just got settled in here."

To all these objections Franklin's answers were entirely unsatisfactory. The land belonged to rushes and frogs; Franklin had seen things he had hoped his sisters would never hear about, and, most fantastic of all, the idea of purchasing the land was not to put it to any use at all, but only to wait until other men had improved the vicinage and the value inevitably soared.

Amasa toyed for a while with the charm of the problem. "We could ditch it," he said. "Maybe build docks. Or run a ferry."

Asa said, "I call it blood-sucking. Why didn't you buy land we could improve, if you had to buy more?"

"Land," said Amoy, "is worth what you can make it yield you. When this Chicago boom is over, the New York investors are going to find that out."

Franklin argued, but it was like talking to children. He grew sarcastic and lost the tepid alliance of his older brother Amasa. Asa too patently forgave him, and his mother was gently sorry about his mistake. So Franklin stuck the option paper in his new hat, clapped it on his head, and slammed his way out of the log house.

He had to come back for supper, of course, with burrs all over his trousers, and he unfolded then his second secret. He had accepted a commission as an adjustor; in harsher language, this meant that he was going to ride all over the district collecting old bills for the Chicago, St. Louis, and Alton merchants, taking a percentage on the collections.

I can hear the irritated rasp of Asa's chair as he pushed back from the table. The girls' eyes widened at their father's unprecedented outburst.

"Now look here, Franklin, that's not a Goodner way. There are two ways of making money; one is producing it out of the stuff God gave us on earth. The other's the leech's way."

Franklin flamed back at him. "It's just the same as what lawyers do, but they charge a lot more for it."

"It takes more brains to be a lawyer," murmured Amasa. "All you need for bill collecting is a hard heart."

"I say it's a leech's way." This is their father's ringing voice. "It isn't that I don't believe in a man's paying his honest debts, but these people out here have got a mighty heavy load to carry. We'll

A Prairie Grove

all have to haul it pulling together. The West has got its back teeth mortgaged to the East, and we can't sell them what we've got, with the cost of transport over the mountains what it comes to. There's no door for us but the New Orleans merchants, and they know it."

"There will be," said Franklin, "when you can sail from the Illinois to New York harbor by the lakes and canals."

So they got back to the five acres of swamp water at the mouth of the Chicago river. When the dispute was all over, the option was to be allowed to die, and the seventy-five dollars written down to loss, without fixing blame.

Franklin became an adjustor and removed to Chicago. That town was going to grow; women would have to come, bringing with them the need for luxury that made business flower. Jogging in to Chicago, the hocks of Washington spattered high with November mud, the wholly deciduous woods barren and the prairies rusty bleak, Franklin saw before his persuaded vision the stone house, the deep stair carpet, the small comb on the boudoir table with the fluff of gold in it.

28

CHANCE RANDELMAN kept coming to the house. He did not know when he had hunted this kind of game in the bosom of a family, and he did not know for certain which girl he was courting. Suddenly Patience looked scarcely older than her sisters; the stove gave her face a pretty flush; she had pretty fingers, and her seriousness had a charm that Chance had never before tasted. She explained to him the mysteries of pearl ash, and he attended with mock gravity; the theory of biscuits did not interest him, but her practice of it was perfect, and this Yankee cooking, this domestic altar of a stove, the forgotten decoration of books on a shelf, piety, and so much mature innocence in a girl who would have been shocked by everything about him, had she understood him—these were the quiet room of Patience. He stood no more than in its doorway still, and he could not decide whether it would be more hard fun to come in or to draw the girl out by both her wrists.

He knew a bird when it was restless for departure, and he understood Delia better than her family, to

A Prairie Grove

whom she was one of the children. He might have had a cruel pleasure in showing her how well he understood her; he could have unmasked her unconcern and, drawing tight the noose of instinct, have made her tremble at herself.

With Rhoda he found himself marching to a tune she seemed to know better than he. She would not meet him one half as often as he wished; he could not say things to her that meant nothing; he had either to advance or retreat. She had not her older sister's touch of prudery, or Delia's vanity. She had more warmth and more candor than either. Her eyes said, her arms said, either I am your wife, or you are a stranger. So they quarreled. He got no more kisses, knowing that by one more he would stand revealed as either a husband or a seducer. Her breasts, proud tender twins, promised rest for him and his; all her body spoke to him, saying, I am woman; how much of a man are you? So under her eyes there could be no courting of her sisters, and when they were alone, he did not make more than a stormy slow progress with her.

If Patience and Delia had known that Randelman was Rhoda's suitor, they would have stayed out of the way. As it was, they tried to cast their spells in quiet without doing anything for which Mary Tram-

A Prairie Grove

ble could look at them with long intent. Silently that well-born lady combated her visitor. He bought his way into the house with stupendous turkeys, with quail, prairie chicken, venison, and duck, and Asa was always honestly glad for his woodman's advice. Asa trusted the taste and sense of his daughters almost boundlessly; what they were too young to know, his wife would understand for them.

Chance Randelman had family; that is, he had half of a family. The Randelmans were South Carolina, and he took the trouble to explain this to Asa and Mary Tramble together. His father hadn't wanted to marry as the family saw fit. Asa clapped him kindly on the shoulder; Goodners feel that you can come-out in your marriage too. But Mary Tramble asked, "But why did they object?"

Melissa Babb, the bride of Broadus Randelman, had been a Tennessee mountain girl. There is no other record of her. But you can imagine the rest. She was young just one spring; perhaps Broadus first saw her barefoot in a brook, or amidst azaleas in flower. If Chance remembered that she smoked a corncob pipe in her old age, he did not tell the Goodners of it.

He had known Tennessee, Kentucky, Indiana, and southern Illinois, in the slow nomadism of the fam-

A Prairie Grove

ily; he could just remember when his own house had had books in it. His father had given him fragments of a distant cultivation, so that when he hesitated, perplexed, over the three Goodner daughters, he remembered the casket scene in *The Merchant of Venice*. But he had a presentiment that he was the Prince of Morocco, destined to open the wrong box. For he knew himself. He had every art that a frontiersman needed; he was much less of a simpleton than Asa or Amasa; he was not afraid of anything physical; he was not entangled in sentiment. But the frontier is a thin strip and a shifting one. Guile like Franklin's could get the better of all Chance's wood wisdom; it would drive him out of his woods in the end. And wherever they could, women made the world as they would like to have it. What a woman's trick those caskets were!

Winter came. All November there was no sun. The woods were sad, only the marshes had life in them, for the ducks and the geese were going over. Randelman had Timothy with him in the cattails, and he taught him to shoot flying and to leave the rank-fleshed mergansers alone and go for the delicate teal and the mallards. As he could do nothing with the boy's sisters, Chance felt a craving to put his hand into this young life that women had made

A Prairie Grove

soft. He felt the pleasure of initiation when at last he got the youngster to enjoy a clean shot through the game's heart. He taught him the cunning of traps and gave him a knife for skinning.

Timothy's hand stopped fumbling; his reserve stiffened into confidence. He learned with an application that his teacher had never seen, but there was something growing in the boy for which Chance had no word. He had hardly heard the name of natural science; he did not recognize abstract interest when he met it, and thought it simply idle curiosity. Randelman threw skinned muskrats to his bitch Letty; the boy wanted to dissect them. Chance let him, thinking the lad's morbid interest would soon flag. He found him just delicately teasing out the embryos from a little deer mouse. So that's it! thought the man, and said, "Want to know about that? Most animals just have them in spring, but mice are at it the year around, if they get the chance. Like people."

"Know about it already," said the boy without looking up. "People aren't my business. Mice are."

December stormed in on the north wind raiding from Keewatin to the Staked Plains. There were three storms that you could scarcely distinguish, following each other with a long animal wail at the

A Prairie Grove

back of their white throats. The first locked up the rivers and devoured the scenery. The second scoured and sculptured the mountains of the first. The third cased the trees in sleet; it cracked tree limbs in its grip and dropped the little ice-freighted kinglets and longspurs dead from its paralyzing grasp.

Only when it was gone and the peace of death glittered marble and graven in the winter solstice did the temperature really begin to fall. The sun came out, but nothing thawed. The beautiful blue dead air lay inert over half the continent. Across crusts like the meaningless floor of the sea the glare made the men look down in pain, as animals will who are hurt by your stare. Nancy and Sybil would come running back sobbing from the privy. The older girls brought the linen in from the line, stiff and glittering with ice. Even Chance didn't come; the snow was too deep for the roan. Amasa said it was warmer in the byre than the house. But the fire roared, and the whole family around it did not feel crowded; they shared seats, and children on the lap were warming, like cats or muffs.

The children liked the widespread disaster that was winter, and even the adults could still laugh at it. "January thaws, you know," promised Amoy. Patience blew on John Paul's fingers; Timothy

A Prairie Grove

sewed on mink skins for his mother with Sybil on his left thigh, her head on his shoulder as she read aloud from her geography. She did not care for geography at all, but she had formed one of the passing unsentimental, unphysical attachments within the family that two Goodners will unexpectedly strike up, they don't know why. All day the three older sisters were given to hugging and comforting each her own chilly upper arms; at night they lay together in their bed in the back room in a mutual happy warmth. In the trundle bed even Sybil and Nancy, who never got on together, slept close as kittens. The boys and Amoy slept in the low loft; Amasa swore when he had to put foot to the floor in the morning. But Timothy had a craving to lie coolly and by himself; he made a pallet on the planks, and the boards under his shoulder blades gave him something he wanted; they said, "Lie straight, take the hard, walk up-wind, see no murk, look in the crystal."

In January, when no thaw came, he went to the river and toiled till he got the snow cleared off a patch of ice. Then in his bulky clothes he lay flat and put his hands edgewise to his temples to look deep in the locked water world. Presently, clearing more patches, he found what he was seeking—the

A Prairie Grove

tiny silver bubbles from the muskrat's snout were fountaining up to collect beneath the ice as one luminous sphere.

Purified by its passage through the water, the oxygen gleamed there and the animal, swimming with his hind feet and his tail, the forelegs held squirrel-like, rose sleek and gleaming with an eager nose to breathe back his translated breath. Then he saw the man shape dark and sprawled above him, bobbed sealwise, and shot with empty aching lungs for his deep suckhole in the bank.

The boy stood up and took the bearings by two willows and a naked clump of kinnikinnick, red switches spearing out of the drifts; he could come back here and break the ice and bait his trap. He was beginning to get the feel of something for which he knew no precise terms. He saw, for instance, that the teeth of the beasts could be written down as a specific dental formula, as his mother had learned at the seminary to identify flowers by their stamens and pistils. He had no books, and did not know the titles of any of those he wanted, but he could see species and families clear as he had seen the ribband strands of the eelgrass in the frozen river. His passion to collect was still juvenile enough, but he also wanted to know.

A Prairie Grove

He couldn't wait for spring, when the ground would loosen and he could dig open the burrows of all the creatures that in the great horizontal scenery dwell underground. The feel of a small wild beast in the hand made his heart laugh, but then he would keep quiet, calming the vole or the shrew. And these little creatures had languages, but their voices were a whisper; no one seemed to hear them but Timothy. They moved so swiftly on the snow that others thought they had seen the shadow of a blowing leaf, but he always saw where they had dived into their ventholes, and thrusting the crust and snow away, could overtake them and pocket them.

Living with field mice, skins of woodchucks, and the smell of mink was hard on the rest of the family, but they recognized that Timothy had some business not theirs.

29

That was the winter of the wolves. In this grove then, on the naked sweeps, in all the sprawling county of Crawford—name for an emptiness—there was not man's way, but wolf's way. They had the last of their nights then; in a little while they would be rounded up in a hunting circle like their own; they would be shot down; they would die on the coming railroad tracks. There was no quarter for them, and they had to take the lead in their hearts and brains. They went out, scarlet rage and fear going suddenly black. They died with their hunger unfed, with the cubs unborn in the swaying bellies.

But there was a time, when the big cats were gone and the deer grown plentiful, when sheep and fowl and calves were first here to be raided, that the timber wolves and the prairie wolves were king for a decade. In the deeply penetrating disturbance of the old biota, kings fell from their thrones, and one species or another, in those unsettled times, might rise from jackal rank to leadership. But dynasty they could not have; they had their hour, and that was all.

A Prairie Grove

The wolf pack was for the most part a family affair. The hunger would drive one pack upon another's bailiwick. Together the two might flee an agonizing fast; then they would catch a third pack up in their flight from torment. But it was not all running; they only ran when there was something to catch. Else they ate despair, and would sit about and weep for themselves like Indians.

When a man is hungry, long hungry, he is whipped. Soldiers will beg, wives will sell themselves; mothers will ask strangers to take their children if they will only feed them. But wolf's hunger is a rack torture, and when the prey is flaired there is no begging for it and no price. Only running then, mile after mile after mile, endurance on fatigue, craving as a whip, and at the end a desperate fight. When the kill went down, an hour was lived in an instant; it seemed as though the fangs had had but a morsel and the tongue had barely lapped blood. One buck to a pack made hunger only grow savagely joyous. It was a collective hunger, such as we know nothing about; there is nothing to compare it to but mob anger; to a mob, one victim may not be enough.

Old hunters' wolf stories are colored till they glare with lies. Wolves were not brave; they were not as cunning as the foxes they hunted; they had the weak-

A Prairie Grove

ness as well as the strength of the herd. Indians did not think much of wolves; I have never read an Indian legend or narrative of wolves eating a live man. But they ate a dead one here that winter, twenty miles south of the grove. When what was left was found in spring, he was known by the diamond on his finger bone as a land shark from Wilmington who had turned a hundred and fifteen people out of Brown County in Indiana. But the wind had got him, and the drifts, and then the wolves. The pack caught his horse twelve miles away; it had strayed off the trace when the rider dropped from the saddle.

They sprang the traps that winter, that Kiercereau and Timothy set, and stole the bait. Or they found the animals that had got caught there and ate them to the imprisoned paw. The twin John Paul ran in to tell of a skulking dog in the twilight; he was more frightened than if it had been a dog. Patience went out with him to see, and what she saw was six dogs that were wolves. The slam of the door sent them flying.

Then they began to make the nights atrocious. That long plaint, generated deep in the throat, held long in the muzzle, wound through the dreams of the half-breed. He had a shack on the Seignelay, a rickety old structure built by some previous trap-

A Prairie Grove

per, that it seemed the teeth of the north wind might crunch. The few who had ever looked inside it remembered a den of a home, with bits of things that he planned vaguely to turn some day to use lying about in dust and rot. The wolves knew his doorstep for its smell of musk and mink glands and squirrel fat, for he sat and cleaned skins there. When he saw their tracks around his place in the morning, he would swear. But now he was dreaming, the moon on his face, his fire almost out. In his dream there were running and pursuit and an aboriginal terror.

Chance Randelman woke up and heard what he called the singing. He had a cabin opposite Catfish Ferry, and so far as I can locate this today, it must have been near the mouth of the Kilimick, where the old Frenchman ran a raft across for the travelers for Chicago. He lived there with Bird, his servant; Bird was a Negro, for Chance was a real southerner who could not be happy away from a race that he despised. Owning Bird was like having a dog, but a dog who could cook and keep house and clean the mud off your clothes. He supplied the welcome home, the fretful solicitude, and the admiration that a woman gives. Bird was afraid of wolves, afraid of ghosts, afraid of bad luck; he had

A Prairie Grove

Chance's superstition for him, so that Chance could reassure himself by mocking the shivering black buck. Fortunately for Bird, he slept dead when he slept; the cold wind of a cry blew through the cabin without troubling him.

The song of the wolves stirred the hunter in Randelman; he lay tingling with unnamed desires. He thought how they spoiled the hunting and hated them hotly. He had once caught a wolf hardly more than a cub, right in the door; he grabbed it by the scruff, got the dog whip off the wall, and gave the rear quarters a long lesson; then he flung the young thief through the door and watched it scud with shamed tail for cover. He never quite knew why he hadn't simply drawn his revolver, but he had liked punishing that limb of hell. His traps belonged to him alone, and that wolf knew it now.

He was a bewildered man, although his gun sight was so steady. He lived, you would have said, like one who knew precisely what he wanted and the short way to getting it. But he was not unimaginative, and he saw the closing of a circle. He had virtues that had been worth life itself in the first stages of pioneering. That was the time when this people, we, these Americans, were cutting a way slow but clean through the hardwood forest and the moun-

A Prairie Grove

tains. That was Boone's age, but the Boone men are sad men now. When there are no savages to slaughter to the glory of the Lord, their virtues sour. Sometimes we have to hang them; sometimes they are only lazy husbands, killing a succession of wives; perhaps the rich ones go to Africa and pretend.

Randelman was young, only twenty-eight that winter; there must have been bloom on him. He had heart to warm and discomfort his selfishness. He had breeding, so that he knew how much of breeding was lacking in him. Where he did not indulge himself, he kept a strict discipline. His first law for himself was liberty; he had never worked in his life, in the sense in which the Yankees meant work, and fences were enough to make him move on. Moving on was in the blood of his kind; they were the ones who went first, but they could never remain where they went. What they did took a courage that only they had, but they did it because it was for them the easiest way out of encroaching responsibility. He and all of them were bewildered people, because they hated the wolves with a Biblical righteousness, yet when the cocks instead of the muzzles cried on midnight, they followed the pack.

He, Chance, would have been over the Rock River and into the Military Tract before this, if the circle were not already closing around him. He had not imagined before that there was any circumference that could bind him, but the linked hands of three girls held him fast. He was a seducer, but he had never intentionally harmed any innocent girl or woman; his had all met him halfway; they expected nothing of him and no better behavior of themselves. They were reckless young animals who had decided to run with the wolves.

But now he heard the damnation and the ever-unsatisfied lust in the pack's voices. He found himself on the other side, and instincts that he had not known he possessed were twined with his own appetites. A door that he could lock on his happiness, a roof wider and holier than this one, a bed made by a white hand—he could have them, for the price of giving his name and losing his identity. He had no illusion that Goodners could be changed; you would have to be one of them under their eyes. He saw how his father had broken with his family; Goodners may live in the south and have other names, and even a marriage may appear illicit to them. He supposed that perhaps his father had looked to them like the weak member of the clan. Which of the girls was the link that you could break?

A Prairie Grove

Mary Tramble crept back to bed from the round of her family and the replenishing of the fire. She got into warmth again, and lay with her cheek serenely on one fine hand, listening to the shuddering misery of the wolf cry. Behind dutifully closed eyes she faced her wolves. She had a literary and a moral mind. She was not imminently nor seriously afraid of fangs; the door was locked, the gun hung over the mantel; she had men about her. It was not wild beasts that she feared. Life has so many dangers in it that you cannot risk trepidation; Mary Tramble Goodner remained calm about her daughters. But she always wanted to slam the door when she let Chance Randelman out of it. She knew too much about women to think that the girls were safe because they slept at home. Woman is never safe from her instincts; when the floodgates of her generosity open she may be swept out of the safest home.

Even what was called a happy life was stern to woman. Mary herself had felt the irresistible invasion of personality that love brings, and pregnancy, and a single devotion to family. These brought their own rewards, but they cost a round price. Simple women do not count it over; this one was not simple; she had will, she had mentality for which the

A Prairie Grove

biology of her career found no employment; at best, it might only be passed on to her children. It flowered also into a delicate realization of life which makes her letters invaluable to me.

Mary Tramble, I see, would never pity her daughters any more than herself, for being consumed by an honorable destiny. To nourish life was the best *métier*. Waste was another thing and not waste wholly was the spent hare that, miles away, under that winter moon, felt the jaws close. Flesh and bones had a long moment of agony; then they became wolf. Tenderness and flight were made into speed and hate and sight in the dark.

30

At last even the beauty of winter was taken down. The ice casing dropped from the trees; the height and the purity were gone from the sky, and the snow departed from the high places and in dark runnels seeped to the low ones, marsh water lying upon old ice that slowly rotted. This was the moment of the great hunger among the beasts, when the hibernators came forth and found nothing green to eat. Lean, they woke to weather colder than when they had waddled to bed. The carnivores, spent, shedding their winter fur, arrived at the mating season; it was just one new hunger to try short cat and dog tempers. The gray fox—there were no red ones here in those days—the big dog gray fox, bit the vixen for her coquetry, but a bite, like one blow, may not be enough. He had to bound half a brush behind her, nipping and panting, till she had had enough punishment. There was no place on the earth to curl up in comfort, no sun or leaves yet, only cold mud and low sky. The beautiful white tips of the buntings' plumage began to wear off. The winter

A Prairie Grove

was old and shabby, and could bring nothing better than an end.

The Goodner children could not be philosophic any longer. The twins complained, and Sybil longed to quarrel with anyone who would challenge her tart tongue. Timothy was sick in his mother's four-poster, and he could not get his brothers to make the rounds of his traps now because fur at this season was of no value. He saw his specimens mauled or rotting, and coughed with continual restlessness. Delia had discovered now that she and Rhoda were rivals—she disregarded Patience; she was angry with Rhoda for her reserve and because the red dress so became her. She knew that she had succeeded in making Chance Randelman long to kiss her, and weather and family conspired to keep her from seeing him alone. The vast, muddy-footed good temper of her father and eldest brother put her out of sorts with all men. But in her adorable young face you could not read the exciting pleasure she found in deceiving everyone and planning their confusion.

Old Amoy took the intensest of endurable heat upon the cap of his knees where he sat in the attitude of a grasshopper up against the fire, cracking nuts. He was the only one of them all not discontented, confined, tired of it, and hungering. How

A Prairie Grove

beautiful it was, he thought, to be just deaf enough so that you couldn't hear ordinary scratches and thumps! To be able to nap in the day, to think of death without horror, to have earned already the rest of your dinners, to have your children tell you what to do and never tell you what they were going to do, to wonder sometimes what had become of all the threats with which you had been kept from life's longest and saltiest voyages—these made up old age. Surprisingly, it was as much a mixed drink as youth had been. But Amoy had learned to down his elixirs neat.

Well, it was a long trip from toothlessness to toothlessness, as far as from Amoy, China, to Amoy in Illinois. He had chosen the forks in the road by the random of whim, and he had been intuitive or lucky. Suppose he'd stuck with the seafaring Goodners of Salem! It had sounded like a fine life in those days; travel and money, merchants and pirates, womenfolk and ladyfolk. But if he'd gone sailoring, some other man would have got Catherine, and somebody else would have raised the finest Merino wool in the United States. He had loaned money to these quarter-deck male relatives of his when the great days of New England's maritime empire were over. That fool war with England had pretty

A Prairie Grove

well spoiled their fun, and he was glad he'd kept his feet dry. True, wool too had spun out pretty thin when the South discovered cotton. When you have a contest between a fine product and a sleazy one, the fine one loses—lingeringly, disdainfully, and certainly.

Amoy Goodner, holding the upturned flatiron between his knees, smashed another hickory shell with a hammer blow, in a neat anger.

His granddaughter Delia got her magical hair, her long, statuelike hips, and the laughter of her quick-lashed eyes from Catherine O'Brien. But she got her sheer fire-worshiping passions from the now silvered Amoy. They were both wilful, but his will now had no sap. He cracked nuts still with relish, but he hadn't the teeth to eat them; the girl came and took a cracked butternut away from him and ate it nimbly.

How he had worshiped the fire through the woman he chose! He had tasted the impish enjoyment of confounding his family beyond Delia's frail powers, when he married his Kate. He had let them agonize over the fear that a Goodner had gone over to Rome, without bothering to tell them that Katie laughed at the priests. Poor old Pope, there were so many things in this world he wasn't allowed to

A Prairie Grove

find out, so many mistakes he might make, so many oceans he could not stop, that it was no wonder his name was Innocent. That's what Kate had said, with her hair tickling his ear and his arm under her.

He could just remember the secrecy, the bubbling, the unquestionable right of it. He had forgotten the deep astonishment, the scar of a treacherous weapon that will be left on any lover who stands by women. The look of her eyes widening and darkening with pain, the spectacle of courage glittering and towering up before you, the final chaos, and the astounding insignificance of the result of it all, tadpole-shaped and uncertain whether to continue this new endeavor of snuffling in air and wailing it out—he had supposed that you could never forget what the bill was like when it came in, but he had forgotten it, serenely. Because women forgive you all those debts.

Well, and now he could feel in his bones that spring was beginning again, all the old ruckus. You never could crack the hardest nuts, and he had had enough of coddling this chimney. They didn't know, when he unfolded himself from his hot corner, that Amoy had decided their winter was over. But he knew that you couldn't hold times and tempers back,

A Prairie Grove

and for his part he would always open the door for them.

So without even his muffler or cap he went and stood in the doorway, bent at the knees, bent at the hips, bent at the shoulders, achieving balance without anywhere being able, any more than an old tree, to hold a limb plumb. He took in a long, wavering breath—suddenly aware that there were not so many of those left to him—and with it in his lungs he tasted what was in it. He saw the haze that was not yet greenness; but only quickness in the high ultimate twigs; he saw ground silver holding a little blue in it. The eaves were dripping and the sun was shining through the drops. He was not so old but that the promise of disturbance and joy was decipherable to him, although not meant for him. It's over, he thought, it's beginning.

He said, "Let's stand the door open for a while, my dears; the wind's turned south. Well, I guess we wintered it out."

3 1

THAT SPRING the island grove was for the last time indeed an island, when the waters of the Kilimick and of the Seignelay rose up in their sullen anger and showed their power. The plows were to come; the old prairie roots and culms would go, and dutiful cereals, manageable and shallow of their hold, would take their place. The ditches of small farmholdings would leech the land. So the great floods would go. At last even the mud would go, with the falling water table of the land, the drying of the sloughs.

But the old accounts, all the early travelers' tales, tell the story of the might of vernal water. "For two days, though in the heart of the continent, our wheels were never once out of water." "A year ago we had passed this way dry shod in autumn, over the prairie grass blackened with fire; then we were put to it to find a stagnant puddle to drink, a spot big enough to wet a heron's foot. Now we seemed like Noah to wander on a watery waste." "Our ox-carts were five days in making seven miles through

A Prairie Grove

the thaw and the muddy sea." "An old man having died in the wagons, we could not find a dry place to lay his body until the end of the third day." "The trace—you could hardly call it a road—disappeared at the edge of our girdled rise of wooded ground as two ruts in the bitter cold and dirty water. We should never have begun our journey at this season, nor would we have done so but for the land fever and the rumor that all the best sites would be secured from the government before autumn."

The sign for water is in all the old zodiacs, whether invented for spring beside the Ho or the Tigris. Before there can be growth and flowering, fruit and plenty, there must be water. This is law, and the writ runs too, along the Ohio and the Muskingum, the Wabash and the Seignelay. In the Old World you have the symbol of the Fishes and the Water Carrier. The Ioway called March the Moon of Frogs.

For the frogs racially remember the watery eras, the age of the world marshes, when the club mosses, great and branched as trees, were showering down the spores that laid the coal measures. Now, first, the swamp tree frogs began to pipe, in the night, and the thin eery creaking stole to the ears of Patience, wakeful and remembering a rocky spring

A Prairie Grove

sweet with arbutus. *Pip-pip-pip*, they called; *creak, crack, crick*. The sound upwelled as a choral of unearthly rejoicing in something pre-Adamite and hostile to his sons. *Peep-pee-yeap*; by day the chanting ringed the grove around, and re-echoing stretched away to the aqueous and lonely rim of March.

Then was the convocation of amphibians, when the many kinds of salamanders mingled at the vast breeding waters. The spotted species in the icy darkness danced their courting saraband, males and females weaving through the shallows, till the little grinning dragon males set their spermatophoric cones, and the females swept them up in the thin cloacal lips.

The frogs were met, by moonlight, in tremulous liquid; the tiny swamp tree frog's throat swelled out, a pearly sack as great as all his body, to pipe the female to him. The green frogs clasped in the long and cold embrace, and when the roe at last was laid, the milt was cast upon the waters, to come back alive and swarming.

The green frogs plucked their 'cello strings; the deep note gurgled in the flood. The bass male chuckling of the wood frogs ran under the long snoring croak of the leopards, and over the swamp peepers' choral soared thinly the wail of the Hylas, the tree

A Prairie Grove

frogs, prophesying rain to come, more rain to fall, and waters still to rise.

The old ice rotted; it rose and melted; it sank and was refrozen, and continually turning in convective thermostat, it ringed the grove with a saltless arctic sea, where the grebes bobbed and dove, and the mergansers and the loons did turns around the isle.

The killdeer came, complaining, slanting in sideways as if hunting for one dry spot to rest their breasts. The spring clouds flew, darkening drowned meadows to a slaty sea. In the stern light the false groves of cottonwood and aspen rose white-limbed and awed. Then the clouds broke, and the sunlight shafted, wanly, to be drunk deep by the black earth, eager of absorption. Beside the cabin door, like Noah's dove, a single bluebird lighted, earth-scorning, and sitting on an upright stump shook out the soft contralto song a moment to the sunlight. When the clouds closed over he was gone.

Secretly the rough-shanked willows round the interior sloughs began to limber, with a yellowing of the twigs that snap off at a touch. Delia, walking in the wind with billowing skirts, broke off a switch and whistled it angrily through the air. She was deeply restless, increasingly belligerent to all her

A Prairie Grove

family. She brought the withe down on her winter-whitened palm, but did not feel the tingle as a pain.

Asa Goodner left his books and walked down through the oak openings and over the wild wet sod, to see what had become of his apple seedlings. The little withes looked dead—frozen and drowned and done for. He scratched them with a horny nail, one, and then another, but they were gone—the delicate Greenings, the brave young Winesaps, the Pumpkin-Sweets and the Summer Queens and Fall Pippins. Only, somehow, he found, the Rambos had survived. Hardy, trusty, lucky, sweet, they had pulled through by a miracle. He remembered where he had planted them, on the higher ground, and how he'd battled with the choking grass and had its roots out all around the Rambo roots. From the first, all the way in the long wagon haul, he'd pampered them. Mary Tramble had opined he thought more of those Rambos than of his daughters; you'd give them, she had teased, the last cupful of water in a desert.

Well, they had their fill of water now, and with sea-blue Goodner eyes he looked west across the receding waste of mud. Another, in that moment, might have owned himself a beaten man, a foolhardy adventurer who had lost the race by running at the

A Prairie Grove

start too fast and far. He was sick enough with disappointment to lean upon his rigid arm, against an oak bole where the bark algas were green with the poisonous-looking verdure of spring at the rank. But Asa Goodner was the sort who tries again—the Sisyphus who defeats the stone and the whim of gods. Before him stretched the sodden prairie, waiting to try him with its might, to dull his plowshare and kill his team. Back of the tender blue of the sky lurked the raw cobalt of August, the drought, and the searing. He had come with ax and fire and share and woman and child. But the untamed continent kept last words to say. It had the buffalo flies to loose upon his cattle, and the ague in its breath. It could send the crows and the pigeons, the prairie chickens and the squirrels, to pick his grain; and like the ill will of Nikanapi, it packed the scorching west wind in its medicine bag. Frailly erect, looking like a hibernator just emerged, in the baggy last of his winter clothes, Asa Goodner stood and stared down aboriginal enemy with an indomitable dream.

Where the bitterns humped in the impenetrable mud world, amidst the stalks of the dead year's weeds, he saw the tender wheat upthrusting through the future springs. Where his drowned seedlings leaned, he saw the good trees rise, wide spaced, well

A Prairie Grove

pruned, scarlet and crimson globes behind clean leaves. I walk there now, in the vestige of that orchard. Now the apple trees stoop like old women who thrust their hands into the pains and hollows of their backs; they lean upon the props we give them. Yet they refuse old age, except its dignity. Each spring they bear their fragile blow, and some of it—a little still—will ripen to the pome, tart and sprightly at the lips. And this grain, today, is high where Asa looked across the miasmal savannah.

Your kingdom, Asa Goodner, your power and your glory. The barn swallows thank you for the barn with the hand-hewn, snuff-brown beams. Swifts thank you for the chimneys that, one after the other, you and your sons raised here. The bluegrass and the orchard grass, the timothy and redtop, dimple and beck in the young wind, clash leaves and whisper *Asa, Asa.*

But the old high-grass went when you broke the virgin sod; the marshes went with the ditches. They locked with you in battle, and you aged each other. Your seed is here. And the wild grass is gone.

32

THE SOUND began before the sunrise, when the light was a violet paling over the stars. And it began out on the world's rim and was picked up, relayed, washed on, and boastfully flung back. It came to the sleeping grove and ringed the shagbarks and the burr oaks round. There were booming surges of this sound that came in, first a crest and then a just discernible trough of silence, closed by another wave.

Some who can remember still how the prairie chicken used to boom have called it blowing, and some, crowing. Others say he tooted, cooed, whistled "between the call of a bobwhite and the hoarse blowing of the nighthawk." Most of the old accounts agree that it rang out, in the rising pitch of *do, re, mi*, as "boom-ah-BOOM." But Bird, the Negro, claimed they "hollered" *Ole-Mull-Doom.*

Ole-Mull-Doom—the challenge thudded, and the bird upon the last tuft of the young springing grass at the edge of the grove rose up and replied to it, swelling out the enormous orange sacs in his throat in answer. He lifted wings halfway, like a

A Prairie Grove

Frenchman shrugging to his elbows, to his fingertips. But this was the opening gesture of a combat dance. Now male pride erected the stiff tail brush till the excited white feathers showed like the cottontail's scut or the snowy hairs on the deer's rump. And male rage lowered the bird's head, where the neck tufts shot up, black and white and conspicuous as a second tail. Between this gorgeous featherwork the throat sacs bulged like painted war drums, crowing the retort to all other males who had the insolence to live. The tympanum resonated till the furious whoop ran rippling with the greater, the composite wave, toward the shores of dawn.

Mirror image of the cockbird's rage, another bird upon another tuft faced east to the first bird's west and looked, no less, a creature of two tails and a furious drum that bounded about on feathered legs. First bird with a rolling gait stamped his knoll till it gave off a dull subthunder to the anger of the living drum. And second bird did likewise. First bird sprang clear of the knoll, in an ecstasy of annoyance, performing thereby the third step in the ancient ritualistic dance of which he knew, though he had never practiced them before, the figures. He whirled around as he leaped, and came down crest to crest with second bird, who leaped and met his rival

A Prairie Grove

at halfway. They whirled about like fencers, backed, and boomed, ran in to close and became a blur. Out of the first swift passage both emerged to boom again, leaving a drift of feathers on the grass.

Five females had come up to watch the sword dance; the dark bright eyes unblinking took it in. The crowing held them thralled; the swelling of the painted throats was glory in their sight. The outcome did not, personally, engage them; whichever triumphed, a gaudy tyrant would possess them, meek in the dust. In their ears was nothing, anywhere, from earth to sky, and south to north, but the booming, filling up the world with the trumpet blast of an instinct that belongs to spring and youth and yet is older than the very senses, older than sight or sound or smell or nerve. Behind the cluster of the hens were other pairs of cockbirds stamping and crowing to attract their notice. And beyond these, far as a chicken could run or heavily flutter in a day, darted and flirted the gross minuet, and the war cries were repeated to the end of timeless morning and the receding rim of the prairie mirror.

On earth between two dancing rivals moved something which was not of earth, which hung threadlessly in the lightening sky. It moved without sound, and the hawk was directly over them. The crowing

A Prairie Grove

throttled in the swollen throats, the gorgeous sacs collapsed, and dull feathers instantly closed over them; the crests drooped, the proud tails were dejected with the counterinstinct of terror; the legs sank and the whole form squattered into the prairie duns and grays and bronzes which the plumage aped to deception. The hawk tilted by, but swirled back on the first astonished cock in a banked glide, and had her talons in his tail before he could scutter. The ground bird flapped and clawed, leaving a welter of his feathers on the earth he loved. But once she got him in the air, the she-hawk was mistress, and her beak was law. Yet this savage deed was brief, and lost in the mating combats, that were their own kind of savagery. The sound of death went up unheard for the booming.

Boom-ah-BOOM—the sun was up. The sun, renewing in the year, was coming to his lordly realm. The tender grass was shooting, sweet grass that the Indian girls once wove in baskets, holy grass with the odor of a woman's hair, that is the first to bloom, gleaming bronze in the young morning with its anthers dangling on the day. Young day, young steppe, life old and young at once—they were all met here, by annual appointment. And met, unknowing, this season for their last in their old perfection—the habitat

A Prairie Grove

unique of ponderous sod and almost flightless and magnificently polygamous birds, of the wild grain and the locust hordes and the sunflower seeds that were the prairie chickens' fare.

In the old biota, the prairie picture, do not look for the framed composition; the prairie scene with its triumphant horizontal bursts frames apart. Every way it suggests infinity—the bottomless loam, the bottomless blue zenith, the unfixable horizon, and the returning circle. Do not ask of prairie Nature that it shall be pretty, for it is male. It had a shaggy hide and a hoarse voice. It had pride, but was not appealing; it never, like a dainty scene, begged you to spare it, and it did not spare the seed of its own loins. Ungovernably its climate flung from drought to flood and back; it mated its children with a propulsive palm. It had an Indian's penchant for the fat, the *gras*—the tons of the wild grain, the mountains of buffalo steak, that are gone. But the prairie chicken, the pinnated grouse, were here still in the childhood of men and women that I have questioned.

And of all the bird families that ever surrendered the sky for a life of gorging on earth's prodigal table, the grouse and all their kind best merit the thick and carnal name of fowl. Heavy with meat upon their breasts, slow to take off on wings evolv-

A Prairie Grove

ing to disuse, amorous as Turks, proliferous and sporting, they tempt the carnivore in man, as they tempt it in the dog and falcon. With their noisy venery they furnish him an outlet for a pent-up laugh. In their turkey posturings and struts, their cockbirds satirize a man, and the scurrying hens make women silly.

So Chance Randelman, riding out that morning across the drying grass, riding the marches of Illinois from sunup to the grove, had no mercy on the chickens. He would shoot them down in spring as gladly as in autumn; they were fatter, to be sure, in fall, but they were so brassy and so game when in the lists of love that he "liked fine," as Bird would have said, to pluck them at the red flowering.

He thought sincerely that he loved the quarry that he struck. He had the hunter's philosophy of kill—that a gallant victim earns the honor of a clean, short death. No hawk tore the body, no coyote jaws enjoyed the dying struggles. Instead, the bullet dealt a blow, neat, almost abstract. An accurate intelligence in the brain of a centaur hunter sent the quarry a death without time—not even time to fear. Man and horse, rifle, bird dog, and lusty bird—they made one whole, for Chance, a perfect synchronization of instincts, skills, purposes, and worths. Mounted, he

A Prairie Grove

was no longer a frontiersman behind the frontier, a man with half of good blood, a lover whose best boast would be that he had never harmed a girl good enough to marry. On the mare's back he felt, as he looked, twice as tall as any Goodner. Letty, the retriever, trotted at his stirrup, adoring as a daughter. He felt extended by his gun, as education extends one man or money another. Armed, he was the king of beasts, in this morning.

He loved a dead bird in the hand, and his lover's hand went naturally to the heavy breast. As he rode he raised a dead brace up, that was lashed together by the stiff legs, and lifting them to the level of his eyes he gave each bird upon its wind-stirred feathers just a light salute of his lips, while he made the mockery of a smacking sound, homage to beauty of a sort. Then he swung the game out and up toward the sun, with a gay and military gesture. In his way, perhaps, he thanked some Master of Life for these lives, and for his mastery of them.

33

If Chance had been there when Asa and Amasa went out to break prairie with a Yankee bar-share plow, he would have laughed to see its gar-nosed blade flung out as fast as the men could set it in, by the proud violated roots. He would never have plowed the prairie at all, but if he had been there to advise them, he would have had them use a southern jumper plow, for you can make it jump uncompromising snags. It was born of the forest era, among a people who planted between stumps and let it go at that.

If he had been there, Chance would have ridden ahead and shot the turkeys and chickens and the rabbits as they sprang up routed. But Chance was absent, at the taming of the virgin prairie. It was Kiercereau who brought the news, and a note in Rhoda's hand. Between the lines, wherein Mary Tramble read that her second daughter had been married at New Buffalo, Rhoda was trying to say that Chance had insisted on an elopement. Mary Tramble saw—as Kiercereau saw—that Rhoda was more in love than

A Prairie Grove

Chance. And to carry her on pillion away had been his way of showing them that he would fling off the cultivating blade from his very roots.

Rhoda did not say where she was going to live, or when she would come to see them, because she evidently did not know. New Buffalo, they knew from Franklin's disgusted communications, was outstripping Chicago and would, of course, become the zenith city of the Great Lakes. But no one hoped that Chance would keep Rhoda in such comfort. Kiercereau supposed that the young fellow would take her back to his camp on the Kilimick, and there have two slaves instead of one. As the little swart man went away from the Goodners' startled home, he pondered upon the strange ways of maids and men. It seemed to him that they had everything to fear from each other, and that the briefer their necessary encounters, the better. He understood foxes and beavers, muskrats and the river otters, but not why men must be such fools.

Goodners as a rule are willing to talk things out, but never their regrets. On these they are taciturn, and Asa and Amasa, who regarded themselves as the most injured parties, being foremost in responsibility for Rhoda, turned to the prairie with a Biblical anger and took it out upon the refractory sod. A

A Prairie Grove

storm was breaking up; blue sky was winning, and the west wind scudded the clouds before it, so that shadow rushed across the grass drenching the sappy brightness with a darker green. The spots of sunshine hounded shadow, leaped the woods and sped across the river and on to the lakes lost in the reeds. The men sweated, and were chilled again when the wind came.

Already sweet grass was in the grain, and the bluestem, the porcupine grass, and the wild rye were shooting. Prairie was late with spring, and when it flowered it did so shyly. It winked with blue-eyed grass and yellow grassflowers, and there were acres and miles of bird-foot violet, with shooting stars, a New World cyclamen, sprung on their tense slim stalks, the shower of blossoms bursting at the top of its trajectory, the petals flaring up and back as if with the wind of descent. Above the silvery carpeting of pussytoes in spring grew little forests of horsetail; they drooped down to the watery hollows in the land, where the wire rushes were just bursting tiny husky flowers. This was the surface of the prairie, a soft fragrant cheek turned to the sun; this was the most passing and innocent vernal aspect, before the coming to full stature, to the war paint colors of final bloom.

A Prairie Grove

But under the sweetness lurked strength, root linked with root to the horizon. They had the intent, those frail flowers, to keep this undespoiled fertility all to themselves. They locked grips, hugged earth as only the truly native can.

The lark sparrows—they are almost a vanished species now around the grove—went chittering in anger before the struggling mules. The ground squirrels at their holes sat up and with retreat secure looked on in curiosity until the earth too near them trembled. The rattlers, lords there from unreckoned time, reared back, lashed out, and fled. Amasa could break their backs with a slap of the oxhide whip, but they were as many as a crop of dragon's teeth.

High overhead, floating dots of dusk on the sunny prairie, the hawks kept watching. They had a sharp eye for this profound disturbance of their hunting ground. They shifted uneasily upon air currents, and wheeled away, and came back.

When noon came, the womenfolk saw that Amasa and Asa were already more tired than they had ever looked before. Asa looked really old, and his smile came delayed. Amasa scowled, as though he had met with something he couldn't figure how to beat. When they went back, Delia went with them to look. There were just two short ribbons of the blackest earth she

A Prairie Grove

had ever seen, turned over to the sun, and not a stone or a pebble glinting in its midnight.

She stood awhile hugging her arms against the wind and watched them at their grinding slow victory. She saw the reeling of the plow and she heard the whip singing above the shouts of her menfolk; it seemed that the mules were on the side of the obdurate wilderness; their sloping, struggling backs were unwilling. And, woman to her fingertips, she found the whole picture brutal and unnecessary. This way, this costly relentlessness that her father and brother never doubted, she doubted. There were men who came home at night to their white front doors in decent streets, handed their canes to servants, and embraced their wives and daughters, without taint of sweat or grime. There was a man who could bring down all that his woman and he might need for their hunger, with one clean shot to the sky. A wild, wind-blown figure, she turned perversely from where her bread would grow.

The plowshare, resisted, tossed, dulled, lying weary on its side while the men rested, drove on after a long breath, devouring an aboriginal purity. It went shearing through the juicy roots of the prairie clover, and clove the sunflower tubers through the meat. With every yard it gained, it ended grass em-

A Prairie Grove

pire. It turned the old campus of the buffalo under, and evicted the deer mice and the meadow mice, the voles and the spermophiles. They would come back and fatten in the wheat stubble, but every year now they would be turned out again.

The land fought back. First the offside mule was lamed with snake bite, then Asa walked off the field with a wrenched shoulder, and the second mule fell forward with a burst heart. But the will behind the plow, collective and racial, could not be broken. Oxen were brought, and another better plow. With a big wheel to run in the furrow and a small one to ride the sod, the plow bit in, Timothy spelling Amasa. The turned turf lay smooth to the light, and the ancient roots began their rot and deep ferment. This way they broke the prairie's heart, an acre a day at the best.

Behind the plow, the seeds began to fall. It was a sound you could not hear, but the noise of thunder is emptier.

When the wild flags were fading on their fat green ovaries, the sack at Amasa's side was empty and the sun was setting. It was going down in cloudy glory that promised rain. Now let it rain, and the sound upon the roof would sing a triumph. For time out of mind, he thought, it had only rained to make the

A Prairie Grove

floods and grow the useless herbs. He gave a last long look of satisfaction at the perfect furrows running to the very mark that he had set. Beyond, against that thunderbird west, was still the fated but unconquered tangle, darkening momently, grass horizon, ebbing sea that would not come to flood again.

34

I SEE the young wheat spring now, and we have corn and barley, the blue alfalfa and the foamy buckwheat flowers, and oats—how beautiful are oats, when the first wavering ranks of green come spearing bravely in the light! I see the mellow earth turned with mechanical perfection and harrowed; I see the patchwork of the fields, purple clover growing where last year they threshed the spelt. The furrows, with the rhythm of waves or music, follow and curve and vanish. They slice away from the bit of an orchard, leaving a tongue of springy pollinating grass under the trees. The orchard with its short bent columns and its rudely vaulted low roof is a rustic chapel in the plowed productive breadth. And when the wheat is coming up, the blossoms fall, dissolve like foam, are swallowed by the earth, gone like departed breath.

So we see it, Asa Goodner, as you planned it. Or nearly as you planned it; you would not understand everything in the grove today. You could not approve it all, and perhaps you would be right. But you un-

A Prairie Grove

derstood growing, and you knew that the bloom must go for the pome to come.

We have to remember back, and with an effort realize that this bounty and these lawns and the dry swift roads were not what you looked at. Your apple trees clung then with thin roots to their life, but in the woods the wild crabs with the great frail paddle-shaped petals, spoon-hollowed and set in stars of five, shone from their thorns at the end of every tangled natural alley of the wood perspectives. In the fall the hard fruits tumble, green as young leaves, coated in a soft wax and bringing back the tart perfume that went on the wind last spring.

Then in your day, Asa, there was a boundary where the sown and unsown met. It was a tension point; man's will met with roots' will. Beyond, in the high-grass, the herbage struggled up through its own bronze ruin. The seasons there had their appointed flowering, their rising levels, and shallowly the spring flowers rooted, deep the autumn grasses thrust after the falling water table of the year. In the sown were all foes cleared away, all but the one good species being outlawed with the name of weeds, the seeds spaced, the turned furrow shading to conserve the dew, order beautiful and intolerant brought into

A Prairie Grove

primeval thoughtlessness. Two beauties cheek to cheek, and nourished by impartial earth.

A seed may not be sentient, but it is a thing alive. Only in the spore, the seed, the first embryonic days of any living thing is so much treasure and future mightily packed. The seeds swelled with the rains, and the thin wary radicles pushed out and shunning light thirsted toward veins of moisture. When they found it, they gave way next to the deep geotropism within them, the pull to earth's core. The black loam absorbed the light as no other hue of soil will do, and light and warmth bespoke the seed and called the seed leaf up. The single cotyledon of the cereal gained the air; the first shoot sprang beside it and day by day unpacked from the starchy kernel the stuff of growth stored there by last year's sun. The tide of chlorophyll, green chemical of manufactory, appeared incredibly out of tissue where no greenness had been. Now this system was established, water and salt passing through the rootlet membrane and sent up, dead against gravity, to the leaves. These leaves spread to catch the sunshine. Forever that energy has poured away into black space, and only earth's blowing film of greenery can trap it. Sun in the wheat leaf altered and rebuilt the raw earth matter carried soluble from the root—the first step to-

A Prairie Grove

ward the bread, light kneading starch and sugar, foretelling all the sweetness of the kernel, the whiteness of the loaf.

But all the eye saw was the running emerald of the wheat field, the blowing sheet of growth fire.

The eye of Asa found it good. In his philosophy life ought to be simple, simple as wheat. Everything could earn its way, harm nothing, and turn out of some account. A man had his way diagramed for him by everything that grew, woman even more plainly. God had tried to make it easy, but men had concocted such a lot of deviltries that they grew all rootless and bootless or let smut into the kernel.

I have seen eyes that I think must have been like Asa's. They are not afraid to look into strong sunlight; it is not that which hurts them, but the miserable things revealed.

When Rhoda rode home alone for the first time, she asked for her father right away. They said he was out looking the wheat over. So he turned and found her coming up beside him.

I suppose they talked as a father and daughter will who are divided now by life and indisseverable by affection. You can hear her ask, "How is it coming?" the way we mortals do when we can see perfectly well how it is going. A little time away from him

A Prairie Grove

gave her perspective on his years. The battle with the prairie had set the wrinkles deeper and just perceptibly turned the shoulders in. And old men's eyes grow paler, as though life lost its color for them.

All I know for fact about what had happened to Rhoda is that they say she came home and kissed them all and didn't say much. "When Rhoda was a girl," belongs to one part of the family stories about her, and everything else to another part. (And there are many stories, for she lived long.) Of course they asked her, "How's it coming?" But, as with the wheat field, the answer was not spoken, for it could be read. The answer is that change cannot be stayed.

Chance, in the cabin opposite Catfish Ferry, had certain notions of comfort, which for her part his wife meant to alter. To Chance the supreme luxury was to give commands and be obeyed in them. Rhoda was docile; her invasion of his rule was by soft means. His diet, till she came, was almost all game, garnished with wild rice and laced with golden whiskey; the meats now were never quite so rare as he liked them. He had the prodigality of the forest-born about hearth fires, and her waking and sleeping in the goose-feather bed were wreathed in wood smoke and tobacco smoke. The house was full of furs and skins; there were only three windows to as many

A Prairie Grove

rooms, and none of them curtained. But though there was nothing to look in but the owls, Rhoda put up bright-patterned stuff that shut out the stars.

To have kept house in this princely kennel in the ways in which she had been brought up, would have necessitated first an eviction, then razing it and building it over. To begin with, Rhoda sent Bird from the kitchen and scrubbed and scolded after him. She thought of the tears of Patience had she been obliged to cook at that crooked and smoky hearth. She thought of Chance and the good she was to this home of his, and was comforted.

To the river weekly now went an astounded but chuckling Bird to perform a washerwoman's needed task. He came to love all Rhoda's clothing like a child's, and laughed to see it blowing alongside Chance's shirts. There had not been a sadiron in the place, till Rhoda brought a pair. As she took neat stitches in her clothes, and ripped out Bird's gross sewing from garments of his master's, she wondered where her next dresses were to come from. She understood that there were Chicago and Alton merchants who trusted Chance no end; everybody trusted him, but Rhoda began sharply to wonder when he ever paid up and with what. There was more to be mended here, she saw, than a shirt.

A Prairie Grove

But, loyal in wifehood, she said nothing when she rode for a visit to the house in the clearing that she still thought of as "back home." When the light was lengthening, she rode away again, laconic and grown to them disturbing and mysterious. But they expected still that she would somehow bring Chance back with her to them. They thought then, our people, in that hard beginning that was yet so deceptively abundant, that you could mate with the wilderness, teach it and tame it and keep it living with you still.

35

IN THE YEAR when the Goodners broke prairie, the public found northern Illinois. Goodners were pioneers, but the public means everybody. It means preachers and lawyers and landsharks, and landsuckers and idealists and knaves. These people were only a few of them fitted to a wilderness life, and they did not come intending to lead one. They came with a rush to found villages—though of course they called them cities—to edit a newspaper before the subscribers got there. And women came. There were girls looking for husbands and schoolteachers looking for schools. They came childless, and pregnant, and nursing, and clucking a covey of children around them, and like the men they took one look at the wilderness and thought how they could change it. Whether you blame them or admire them for the domesticity of their souls, you have to remember that they were all propelled between the shoulders by predestinarian forces. Thrust west, or running to outstrip the thrust, they saw and thought and acted as they were accustomed to do.

A Prairie Grove

So would you. You like to think that if you had to live in Basutoland you would still be a good American and never let down decent standards of living or rational thought processes. This is just the way people felt when from the prairie sea they raised the island groves on the horizon, and brought to them a Pennsylvania Dutch mentality, a 'way down Maine mentality. Herkimer County Shakers, Chester County Quakers, Baltimore Catholics, people who knew Emerson by sight on the streets of Concord and thought their judgments permanently elevated as a result—all these pietists knew God wanted them to get first into virgin prairie and sow the only good seed.

When a great and seemingly simple event occurs, you usually find that it took the concurrence of many forces to make it possible. The country had just gone through a terrific boom and panic. In July of 1835 it cost an eastern workingman twenty-one per cent more to live than in April of 1834. By October, 1836, everything he bought cost sixty-four per cent more. We began to have labor troubles, and a dangerously radical element agitated for the idle existence of a ten-hour day. There were strikes in Philadelphia, Hartford, Boston, Trenton, Washington, Natchez, St. Louis, Cincinnati, and Louisville. A perilously

A Prairie Grove

popular and left-leaning president was, of course, indirectly responsible for the way that this succulent ham of a country was hurtling to the jaws of Cerberus. The money inflated like a bladder burst in 1837, strikes ended (always a sign of coming woe), and the public could no longer be held back from the westward exodus. Although Henry Clay tried to discourage this draining of cheap labor from the east, by holding western lands at the high price of a dollar and a quarter per acre, he does not seem to have succeeded when he commanded the billows to stop rolling.

Thousands went west by the Erie Canal; passage was so slow, one old woman has told me with a chuckle, that the children used to get off the canal boat and run alongside to pick apples in the orchards. The canal had been completed at the expense of the taxpayers of New York, but it was only a hole in their pockets. It still had to be paid for, and everyone who sold his lands and went west cheapened the value of the New York farms. So they got aboard the bandwagon—the farmers who owned those orchards—and when they got out West, whether they felt better or whether they felt stung, they wrote back home and urged the conservative to come after them.

A Prairie Grove

Advertising looked west; it flooded the distressed industrial cities with persuasions. Margaret Fuller found that God was on the prairie just the same as on Boston Common. Gasped the editor of a Chicago paper, "This town is rapidly filling up with strangers!"

Four hundred and fifty vessels arrived that year in the mouth of Chicago's reedy river; docks built out from the swampy land (the option on which had wrenched free and fluttered from Franklin's hands) received them. In 1836 not a bushel of wheat was exported in northern Illinois; four years later ten thousand bushels would leave those docks in a season. Much of it would go directly to Europe; the golden stream of American wheat drove the European peasant out of business, so he had to come to America.

If you did not come by lake boat, you could go down the Ohio and up to St. Louis by river boat. This craft was considered a floating palace; red carpets, brassbound, climbed the stairs; ladies saw themselves in mirrors wherever they turned, so that the crowd was skilfully exaggerated. The breadth of the river and its height in flood gave one the sense that God had opened a splendid highway for America's manifest destiny. One sailed down Jordan to the land of Canaan.

A Prairie Grove

From St. Louis the stagecoach took you through dust or mud in an aura of mold and horsehide to the edge of frog song, the beginning of thirst, and the land where there is never anything around the corner.

That first summer the Goodners and the prairie grove enter recorded history. I can identify them by three unmistakable references. Ebenezer Wellcomb was a circuit-riding preacher who left his prosy memoirs so squarely in the middle of early bibliography that you have to read them. The Lord enabled this his servant to be right on all occasions, and as he had a habit of pointing people out like an old prophet, he refers to the Goodners by name as a family whose hospitality he enjoyed, but one with a deplorable lack of godliness. As it seemed to him, they were unaware of the perilous situation of their souls. Goodners have souls and know it, but they seldom refer to them. The Reverend Ebenezer Wellcomb turns up in Goodner tradition as a character of comedy, one who distressed and embarrassed them as much as he secretly tickled them.

They are so affable, these Goodners, you would never suspect how hard it is to crack them. They tolerate pontiffs and swamis and Marxists, and they read books about them and have these on their library shelves. It seems hard for a swami to believe that, having heard, they will not follow; he declares that after all they are a shallow people and material. But the truth is that their faith is so firmly rooted in their courage and independence that it is a rocky task to convert them from it.

Ebenezer Wellcomb had arrived, as he tells, exhausted with prairie heat, his horse maddened with buffalo flies, and both of them thirsty as dust. At first he was delighted with the sympathy and solicitude he received, but he was not happy about Asa Goodner's natural religion. Asa loved cherishingly to repeat, "The groves are God's first temples"; he walked beneath his oaks and felt this with all his heart. But Ebenezer Wellcomb appears to have smelled pantheism, and the next morning he spurred his horse into the gadflies and the shimmering wide heat waves.

Eliza Tuttle's autobiography is a foundation stone in the early history of western Wisconsin. She was an Englishwoman to the end of her days, though she lived sixty years in America. She did not like New York City and almost exhausted her opprobrious adjectives on it; when she saw Chicago, she was very nearly speechless. As she journeyed west in a dearborn, with a husband beginning to shake with ague (she attributes this to the unwholesome humors of

A Prairie Grove

Chicago), her situation was really pitiable. She had probably been cheated on the horses; the driver did not in the least know his way, had lost the Galena trace, and dragged the poor woman and her sick husband through sloughs and over grass hummocks for a whole wasted day.

"It was almost sunset when a beautiful grove of trees rose out of this desert, and a beckoning plume of smoke betrayed a human habitation. My heart beat fast with hope, but so many had been my disappointments that I could not but reflect upon our melancholy predicament. What manner of the human race awaited us here in the wilderness? Would we again be leeched for our money, treated to rude Yankee contempt, and forced to sup on 'Johnniecake' and fried pork? But we were in no position to select our lodging for the night; unless we preferred to remain on the open prairie, exposed to unwholesome exhalations and serenaded by the dismal raving of the prairie wolves, we should be obliged to shelter beneath the unknown roof there under those trees.

"The reader who has thus far followed our chequered fortunes in Yankeeland will judge with what astonishment I found myself made welcome in a house which, although rude, was spotlessly clean and even boasted the cultural attainment of books. These people called themselves '*New* Englanders,' and indeed I could find it in my heart to call these good

A Prairie Grove

folk germane to mine. My husband was at once given every comfort that the primitive surroundings allowed, and I was so relieved by the sense of home and decency about me that I gave way at last to tears in the arms of the lady of the house."

The Ohmites were a band of Pennsylvania Germans led by Father Georg Ohm, in search of free soil and God's grace. It is not clear why these were not available at home, but either the neighbors frowned or religious leaders lack originality and have all to begin with an hegira. The Ohmites walked the entire distance from southeastern Pennsylvania to the Pecatonica. Only a week from their destination, when they arrived at Goodner's Grove they were a weary band of the chosen in the world of what they called the Gentiles. Their few wagons containing seeds, bedsteads, sick, and old were allowed by Asa to draw up in the shade of the great oaks, not far from the well.

"The sound of our hymns rising through this grove of trees saluted our salvation and good fortune." Long did the grove remember them, for when the Ohmites departed they had somehow left behind a legacy of buffalo bugs, emerged from their carpeting and bedding, and if ever I write the entomological history of Goodner's Grove, the periodi-

A Prairie Grove

cal outbreaks of *Anthrenus scrophulariae* in attics and horsehair trunks must make a sad item in it. Plowing tamed the terrible prairie flies; the burrows of their larvae are cleft and dried. Buffalo bugs have another way with them; they travel our roads and live in our goods and do their work while we forget them.

The trace by usage became a road of sorts, two deepening ruts, a beaten trough that grooved lower as the surrounding grass grew taller. The squeal of the hubs seemed to Asa's family continuous; I am only glad they cannot hear the Sunday flood of traffic on the paved highway, or see the trailers wagging by on summer week ends.

For now we have to rush on demon speed to get to a place where there is silence enough to shout in. Our elbows are worn with rubbing; we have so many neighbors that we come to ignore all of them. Then, Rhoda reported that the old Frenchman was making twenty trips a day at Catfish Ferry. Chance, the family gathered, was cursing this immigration and threatening to remove, horse, gun, dog, slave, and woman, into the Military Tract beyond the Rock River. At the thought of Rhoda in the country that Black Hawk had so recently harried with the scalping knife, Mary Tramble's head trembled.

For herself, she was growing older, and felt it,

A Prairie Grove

and felt the warmth that other women brought in their coming. It sustained her to be wiser and sustaining, to hold in her arms and comfort a woman nearly beaten by the loneliness and the space.

Then one day, when the thrush had fallen silent for the summer and the cicadas had begun to run their buzz saw, Burt Millerand drove up to the north end of the island with a paper fresh from the land office, titling him to a tract that marched with Asa's. He and his wife and sister and six children lived that summer in their wagons, as the Goodners had lived the year before. The Goodner children went to play with the young Millerands, and over all their voices rang the axes and the ripping sound of trees falling.

Nothing was different in the log house or under the burr oaks but the feeling of the air; it had neighbors in it. Mary Tramble and Patience enjoyed being able to lend to and advise the new womenfolk. Amasa was filled with agricultural and architectural theory, and when Burt Millerand, a self-confident man, would not listen to him, Amasa gained the ear of Burt's sister Jessie, who attended so well that she obviously meant to be the wife for him.

So root was beginning to link with root; the new seed had fallen. The first crops were rushing up,

A Prairie Grove

nourished on an untouched fertility. Corn had been planted after the wheat, and now for the moment the wilderness animals were drawn by the astounding new biological fact of the growing granary. The ground squirrels had never tasted such a banquet; the fox squirrels left the woods for the fields. Rodent teeth gnawed and stripped, and the prairie chickens came like domestic fowl to profit. As the corn ripened, paroquets, tropically green and gaudy yellow and orange, flocked in the field to rasp with hooked bills and talk with raucous self-congratulation as they fed. The Goodners could not keep these pests away; Chance came and helped shoot them from the fields; Delia loaded his guns and handed them to him as fast as they were emptied—flushed, laughing, and flattering at his prowess. But no losses diminished the paroquets, the prairie chickens, and the squirrels. And yet it appeared that there would be harvest enough for all. In its grand impartial bounty this America, this continent, put her man child and her wilderness offspring each to a flowing breast.

36

I HAVE BEFORE ME materials that I gathered with the intention of one day writing a biography of Timothy Goodner. For the records of natural science in the early midwest are as alluring as they are sparse. We have Audubon and Michaux, and Thomas Say had taken a tentative and somewhat Philadelphian sniff of our air. There are mad Rafinesque collecting the shells at the Falls of the Ohio, and Thomas Nuttall drifting lonely as a curlew along the Great Lakes in a trip of which there is no longer any clear record, and you have Bradbury's *Travels* (a collector's item, that) and Lesueur after fresh-water fishes, and George Engelmann riding the Illinois prairies searching out its marsh flora. And Timothy Goodner, a boy still, but at twenty already a Smithsonian correspondent. Four years later he had left the island grove first for Colorado, and then for California by way of the Isthmus of Panama, and there came an end to the specimens sent from the prairie sloughs and the oak openings to Copenhagen and Berlin and Paris.

A Prairie Grove

I have a letter from Petersburg before me; Ledebour is asking Timothy to collect under authority of the Tsar in Russian America. The passport—my best treasure—stamped with the double eagle of the vanished empire, crackles as I draw it from the tattered envelope. I have the photostat of a communication from Sir Richard Owen who wants "some of your American marsupials" to dissect; (he is talking, in his way, about opossums). In other letters—copies mostly—Agassiz asks Cope for sturgeon and Cope asks Goodner for them, and Brünnich wants gallinule and tern eggs, and skins of rails and phalaropes and Bartramian sandpipers, both sexes to be in full breeding plumage.

But I am less lucky than I seem, for the self-documented portion of Timothy Goodner's life only begins after he had quit the island grove, not again to gather patient testimony of its changing forms. For he returned only as a visitor to a family grown vain of him—who talked with the great at Washington, and was given a room and desk as soon as he entered the rich Philadelphia Academy, and ordained, under seal, to be the naturalist with the Oregon boundary survey.

Their Timothy was the vanished boy who had filled the house with the odor of muskrat, and had

A Prairie Grove

brought home the bird's nest roofed over with thistledown out of which, to the horror of Patience, three naked baby mice had squirmed onto her breadboard. But they accepted with an unsurprised pride the Timothy who came to say good-by to them before he went to Oregon; I have the yellow bit of pasteboard that shows him at that time, with his gun and his fur cap and his mustache drooping over a young mouth.

While Goodners tolerate and defend the no-account among them, neither are they astonished when they have bred distinction. When in after years they took the theater tickets she had sent them and went up to Chicago to see Sybil Sorell, they recalled indulgently that she always had been a histrionic child, fond of her mirror and her moods. They spoke of this obliquely, dining at Franklin's elegant home on aristocratic Wabash Avenue, because his wife, a Fleming of West Newton, was morally embarrassed by such a sister-in-law.

Amidst all the worthless letters, the diaries kept by Amasa's daughter who took herself so seriously and was so unimportant, the account books of Asa's horticulturally perfect and financially thin-soled apple business, there is not a scrap of reminiscence by Timothy Goodner. If he had lived to the age of remember-

A Prairie Grove

ing, he might have set down something about those years when there was only the log cabin in the grove and all the birds were still there. But as it is, I have almost nothing to go on, and I long ago perceived that the biography will never be written.

That would have had to be a severely historical work, in deference to the scientist that Timothy became. But my Timothy of the virgin prairie can never be authenticated, so he must go unsung or be evoked out of what I know of a boy's watching and wondering and finding out.

I can walk in his footsteps, conscious that I am treading zoologically classic ground (though it is a bit like visiting the shore of Piraeus hunting for Aristotle the marine biologist). Deep in the woods there are sloughs still left, shrunk to tiny Arals and Chads, for Asa's crack willows have pumped them shallow as he meant them to, and now they overhang the stagnant water and cast green darkness on it. These are frogs' province, and when my footstep shakes the soggy earth, they raise the signal of abrupt silence, and the herons understand it and are sailing heavily away above the trees before I get there.

In the years I have known the sloughs that were once greater and were Timothy's, I have listed twenty-six species of marsh birds. But there was a

A Prairie Grove

fresh-water avifauna in his day that does not return. It moved with the seasons, from the prairies to the pampas and return, with a last crying in the wide interior marshes and a storm of wings when the rails and the plovers and the sandpipers settled on the black sickle that is shore between windy water and whistling grass. On the air then the husky and the plaintive blent, voices first-American, aboriginal, and, it would seem now, alien.

Living thus, between the linked continents' two mountain chains, the birds were a half-secret society in which were members seldom seen along the coast, species, like the black rail, that had become rare almost as soon as they became known. I have handled Timothy Goodner's specimens, in an eastern museum, of the wary old hen rail and three dusky chicks. They lie as skins now, gutted and limp, labeled in Latin in one of the sliding drawers that reach to the ceiling. What was the sky like, Timothy, that day your heart leaped to see them? Did you hate to shoot them, yet know you must? For Bachman and Swainson and Audubon himself would cry aloud with pleasure to see and touch this *Creciscus* that had not been collected since Gmelin named it from Jamaica in 1770.

It is late now, well-nigh too late, for the lost life

A Prairie Grove

of the continental heart. Some saw it, briefly, and remember; they tell us that ducks that are driven now to breed in Canada then nested on the Kilimick; the whistling swans went over in a cloud, and the cormorants flapped up the Seignelay in flight formation, black against old sunsets embering into night. Those were the days of the golden plovers pausing to rest and drink in my sloughs, in spring on their way from Patagonia to Ungava; even Timothy never saw them in fall, for they take a different route for their southward journey and from Arcadia launch across Atlantic waste without ceasing their wing beats till they see green Guiana rising from the Caribbean.

The bitter salt marshes of the coast had nothing more beautiful than the king rail by the sweet waters, or the Florida gallinules, color of a threatening sky. Over the reed lake where the Ottawa guides had led Du Gay astray, the black terns skimmed swallow-wise above their floating nests, with piercing cries. Wary, graceful, tender, the long-billed curlews followed the whistling leader and came down, with folded wings and legs depending daintily till the marsh grass received and concealed them. The hiding Timothy must have seen them as they emerged,

A Prairie Grove

at a mincing run across the soppy sod to the brown waters' edge and, in little ranks, sipped like communicants of the dark water.

I never see the phalaropes, these days—not in this countryside, at least. But they were here in Timothy's times, and I wonder what he made of their strange ways. I hear that it is the female that wears the brilliant plumage and does the courting, and that she is polyandrous as an island queen. They fear that the Eskimo curlew is extinct now, and the sand-hill crane is going.

The cranes are mentioned in any full account of the prairie days. "The cranes were always first back when the spring came." "They stood almost as tall as a man, but they were hard to see, because they seemed to melt into the prairies and the twilight." "They used to keep a sentry while they were feeding on the arrowhead, so you could never get at them." "All of us farm boys knew the sand-hill cranes, but we couldn't find the eggs no matter how we looked."

But Timothy found them, and he says, *Trans. Am. Philosoph. Soc.*:

"Often, in the night, when they are migrating, these paludicoline birds proclaim their advent by the trumpeting that seems to shake the air for miles about. When daylight comes, we see them traveling

A Prairie Grove

in pairs even so early in the year. Their food at this season consists largely in the hips of the prairie rose, which all sorts of animals as if by common consent first allow the long winters to mollify before they will touch them. The cranes habitually stalk, with some majesty and yet no little ludicrousness, over the bare plains, gathering their manna, but nothing is more difficult than to approach them. With the wariness of old prairie scouts they set sentinels to guard their flocks, and, being mounted on their long legs, they stand almost as high as a man and by their telescopic eyes are enabled to see even farther. I have often, however, watched their mating dance, from a concealment of old cattails and in early spring, just after dawn has broken. Nothing is more singular and yet moving than to see them prancing about, lifting their heads, or suddenly lowering them to the ground, hopping and bouncing, with half-raised wings, crossing and recrossing each others' paths, until, their speed increasing, they become a blur of bouncing balls."

I think, from the chronology I have worked out for Goodner's life, that this must have been written from the narrow cell-like room in the Smithsonian, where the books shut out the light of the dusty slit-like window in the absurdly medieval tower. The last that I can learn about sand-hill cranes on my prairie is what I have heard from a man old enough to have

A Prairie Grove

looked at Lincoln in his coffin when it rested in Chicago Courthouse. In the 'seventies, he says, he saw a single bird and occasionally two and three together flying high above the city and making off to the north.

Already then the long freight trains were shunting on the prairie, and southward just over the horizon there was a din of hammers and an inhuman clash of metal where the steel mills were going up. And Timothy Goodner lay dead by Cape Mendocino, in sound of the sorrowful breakers, where west at last comes to an end, and there is nothing beyond America, our home, but alien east.

It had to be—the shrinking of the slough, the tilling and the fencing, the shuddering bang of the freight cars, the shriek of the mill. Many good things have come this way; there is no weariness now like the weariness of breaking prairie; children do not have to die, without a doctor, in the lonely house; there is no danger—and no hope—of loneliness. Mire and ague are gone. The wind blows dry across the clean, plain palm of Illinois.

But once it cupped the grassy sloughs, and treasured the hidden lake where the eel grass and the wild celery fed the waterfowl millions. Something went

A Prairie Grove

away, step by step, first with the buffalo, then the elk, then the prairie chicken and the clamoring, prancing crane—something that was ample and native and dark, like the first loam and the slough water.

37

THE LAST GREAT FLIGHT of the passenger pigeons recorded from the island grove took place when Rhoda's child Flint was ten years old. I know this because there is Flint's letter written to his Uncle Timothy in California. They found it among Goodner's papers, and it says,

"Dear Uncle Tim—

You aught to of been here to see the pigeon we been having. Mother says there was more the first year they came here. I don't see how there could of been. Bird and I shot till our guns was all hot. We been eating pigeon pie till we are sick of it. Peple came from all around lots we never saw before. Some boys that did not have any gun but pertended they did would pick up my pigeons. Uncle Am said there was plenty for everbody but he is always so easy goin. Old Milerand drove in his hogs the third day to get fat on the dead birds. . . ."

The pigeons did not come every year to the grove, but only at rare and unforgettable intervals. They came when the mast in the Michigan forests gave

A Prairie Grove

out. Alexander Wilson calculated that a pigeon daily ate half a pint of acorns or beechnuts, and that a flock consumed seventeen million four hundred and twenty-four bushels in a day; Audubon makes it eighteen million. Wilson said that he saw a column a mile broad, every bird in it moving at the rate of a mile a minute. He watched it for four hours, which means that at his conservative estimate of three pigeons in a square yard, the ribbon of wings was two hundred and forty miles long and contained two thousand two hundred and thirty million, two hundred and seventy-two thousand passenger pigeons. This was but a single band, and of these birds not one today is living.

They are so gone that all we hear of them is fabulous. Alexander Wilson was standing one day at a pioneer's door when there was a tremendous roar out of the sky; the sun was so instantly darkened that he took this happening for a tornado and expected to see the trees torn up. "It is only the pigeons," said the frontiersman. Audubon saw a hawk pounce on a pigeon flight; the birds beneath it plummeted almost to earth like the funnel of a twister, and every bird coming after them executed the same figure, dashing into the vortex and by an unseen force shot out of it again. Everyone speaks

A Prairie Grove

of the roar of the wings; it plowed the forest boughs into billows. Their droppings fell like shot through the leaves till the ground was covered with them, and the voices forever called upon each other. Imagine the tender contented throaty plaint of the barnyard pigeon amplified by a million voices to a portentous crying thunder torn with the speed of flight. Imagine all your county under forest and all that forest one vast pigeon roost; in such quantities they nested or they rested.

If the evidence lay only on the word of a few, it might not be credible, but the agreement among the skeptical and the rivals is too telling. "The boughs of the trees were constantly breaking under the weight of the birds." "You could hear a pigeon roost miles away." "It was the grandest sight I ever saw to watch them streaming across the sky." "The sun was dark for hours when they went over."

They say that their wings flashed in the sun; the soft rose breasts, the delicate blue heads, the wings changeable green and blue and bronze all had pearl-like luster. The luster is gone from the sad museum specimen that looks at a curious public with a glass eye. But there is Audubon's plate, painted from the life with every nacreous gleam of a pinion, and the dour soul who is embarrassed by Audubon can read

A Prairie Grove

the testimony of the cautious Wilson, who makes the pigeon sound as though Audubon's brush had understated it. Such a head-shaker may not want to believe anything that a mere writer would write, like James Fenimore Cooper, but he will have to accept the numbers and the might of the passenger pigeon when told of them by those who suffered from them and so could not love or extol them. "The whole forest was like one vast chicken house; it smelled like it and sounded like it." "Sometimes they would be gone for years, and then they would come back when the nuts were plopping. They would clean up the woods of everything edible and turn their attention to the farmer's corn. In an hour they would ruin him."

I have just Flint's letter to go upon, and it would hardly make an item in a serious ornithological survey of Goodner's Grove, but Rhoda Goodner could not have heard the pigeons coming without feeling their shadow forecast upon her heart.

Hers was the last tragedy in a tragic summer. There was a saying that the first crops that grew so lushly from the virgin soil ran all to leaf, and that the grain was sick. At first the Goodners thought they had the "bread sick" from eating the unwholesome grain, but they saw at last that the prairie,

A Prairie Grove

outraged and angered, was shooting down these mortals with its final arrows. From ancient boggy sod it loosed its malarial and enteric fevers so that Asa was doubled up with an "ague cake" in his side. Patience was shaken with chills, and Timothy suffered then the injury to his heart that was to fell him suddenly in far-off foggy Humboldt County. There was a black mist on the horizon, and the wild sunflowers just beyond the broken land looked far away in the illusory shimmer of the heat. This the Indians had understood, how all things could drift apart on the prairie, dissolve under the sun and float in the day mist so that they seemed cut from earth.

The mornings would wake enchantingly, a little dew still in the shade, and though the birds were mostly silent now, the flickers and the bluejays did their best to be musical for an hour. But by eight o'clock the world was already blazing and intolerable. It was an era in which cool and scant clothing was unthinkable, and will and stoicism surmounted the tortures of the tight basque and the ample skirt. But the heat drew iron wires about the head; the arrows flew. Elizabeth Millerand was down, two of her children were ailing, and Mary Tramble came and went with broths and possets and cherry-bark infusions. Only Delia seemed somehow magically

A Prairie Grove

untouched, more than ever radiant, more than ever absent from the house. Much of her time was not accounted for, and amidst so much sickness her comings and goings were not watched. Only afterwards were they noticed and understood.

The prairie withered though the sky was humid. The sun got up and peered through the jaundiced blue where the dust began to gather. Far off, the grass was burning, and the smoke did not roll away but hung there in gloomy pillars; it smelled of burning humus, and somewhere in it there curled an odor of roasting ghostly and savage. A wind like a fever blew the mists away, and clear honest sunshine, flaming and terrible, scorched the clearing between the oaks. Now surely the last dampness was baked out of this unfathomed soil; surely the last arrow was shot. The ague melted away out of the weary bones of Asa; Patience got a little color. The twins played in the scant shade, for the hickory leaves were beginning to fall without ever having turned to gold. John Paul and Nancy came in looking both flushed and white and Mary Tramble felt their foreheads, no longer damp under the soft hair, but burning.

Eight days later John Paul was dead of bilious

A Prairie Grove

fever, and Nancy died the next morning. They were buried on the following day in terrific heat that made all eyes look scorched. Rhoda and Chance were there, and Rhoda stayed with her mother.

The second week in September a wind rose in the night and stripped the last of the hickories bare. In the morning the sky was blue and chill and warblers were being flung through the woods on the clear storm blowing from Lake Superior. The prairie, gone early to seed in the heat, was suddenly beautiful with the down of its numberless composites, and in the woods the haws turned color, it seemed almost overnight. You could hear the crows and jays and grackles and the big-crested flycatcher all shouting above the wind, but the young wind tore their calls away. It was a day for running, for letting the hair free. That was how they saw Delia for the last time, before the woods swallowed her.

It was Bird who came to tell Asa. He scraped and wept a little and vowed his own fidelity to Rhoda, and it was Asa who had to put the fact in words, in a question, to make sure of it. Yes, Randelman was gone and Miss Delia with him. Asa walked away from him and stood a long time looking at his fields before he found the strength to tell Rhoda.

A Prairie Grove

He was telling her when the pigeons came. Without warning the cloud, not yet arrived, shook the air and passed over the sun like a shadow on the heart. Rhoda went to the door away from her father and looked up with blind eyes at the river in the sky. So wilderness had shaken and darkened her life; so it must pass. In that moment she was cut down, but she was hardy and the seed was in her. She would prevail like the little Rambo trees, when lawless flowering was frostbitten and blackened. Still the pigeons kept coming, a winged crying torrent, and, standing straight, she shaded glittering eyes with her hand to watch their passage. Her pain forecast our loss; we should have known that desire of it would drive the wilderness over the last border.

That year, that time when the pigeons went over, no one in the grove, out of some Goodner sense of fitness, fired a shot. The flying river shed no drop, though it was four days and nights in passing, thinning sometimes, coming again to flood. It went on into the autumn, south as the sun went, with the shortening days, and inevitably it ended; a sky meek now without death or portent in it was clear of the great horde. The last feathered arrow was spent and the last abundance vanished; the medicine bag is empty, and the year, the *annus mirabilis*, is over.

A Prairie Grove

The seed is in, fateful and indomitable; we have populated where we have slain. Still sometimes when in fall or spring the wind turns, coming from a fresh place, we smell wilderness on it, and this is heartbreak and delight.

BIBLIOGRAPHY OF SOURCES*

GENERAL BIBLIOGRAPHICAL WORKS

Buck, Solon Justus. *Travel and Description, 1765-1865.* Illinois State Historical Library, *Collections,* vol. 9. Springfield, 1914.

Rusk, Ralph Leslie. *The Literature of the Middle Western Frontier.* 2 vols. New York, 1926.

* These works, selected after a careful attention to some one hundred and fifty books and articles, indicate the sources of much of the historical, ethnological, scenic, and biological background. But even more the bibliography is intended to serve those who might wish to pursue some line of inquiry farther. Were all the titles in the existent bibliographies of Indian and pioneer life in Illinois as satisfactory as they appear, it would not, perhaps, be so worth while to compile a fresh list. But in the long preparatory search by the author he discovered so many references that came highly recommended or had promising titles to be thin or worthless, for his purposes at least, that it is possible a service may be rendered by collecting together the really rich sources. These were almost all discovered in the libraries of Chicago, namely the John Crerar, the Newberry, Chicago Historical, Chicago Public, and University of Chicago libraries. The author acknowledges gratefully special courtesy shown him by the Crerar and University of Chicago. The Library of Congress has kindly loaned a few volumes not elsewhere to be procured.

A Prairie Grove

ABORIGINES AND FRENCHMEN IN ILLINOIS IN THE SEVENTEENTH CENTURY

ALLOUEZ, CLAUDE JEAN. *Narrative of a Voyage Made to the Illinois.* In French, Benjamin Franklin (ed.). *Historical Collections of Louisiana,* part 4. New York, 1852.

    Father Allouez was one of the most reliable and lovable of all the early missionaries and deserves to be far better honored and read than he is.

BECKWITH, HIRAM WILLIAMS. *The Illinois and Indiana Indians.* In *Fergus Historical Series,* no. 27. Chicago, 1884.

CHARLEVOIX, PIERRE FRANÇOIS XAVIER DE. *Letters to the Duchess of Lesdiguières.* London, 1763.

——— *A Voyage to North America.* Dublin, 1766.

    Father Charlevoix, coming later than the first *voyageurs,* gives excellent perspective and aloof judgment upon the events and personalities of the first contacts of Indian and European life in the Illinois country. He was also a very fair amateur field naturalist, which makes his accounts especially pertinent for this book.

COX, ISAAC JOSLIN (ed.). *The Journeys of René Robert Cavalier, Sieur de La Salle.* New York, 1905.

    La Salle, of course, is the *beau idéal* of the explorer-chevalier. See also Francis Parkman.

CROGHAN, GEORGE. *Journal.* Burlington, N. J., 1875.

    This relates to a captivity among the Indians in Illinois in 1765.

A Prairie Grove

FILLEY, WILLIAM. *Life and Adventures of Wm. Filley, Who Was Stolen by the Indians,* etc. . . . Chicago, 1867.

Accounts of Indian captivities would in themselves form a fascinating bibliography. Many are unreliable even upon a casual reading, but the apparently true and the palpably untrue still agree upon many points and in some ways they throw more light on normal Indian life than do the ceremonious visits of European soldiers, missionaries, and other guests free to depart. See also, in this section of the bibliography, Croghan, Hunter, Tanner.

FORD, THOMAS. *A History of Illinois.* Chicago, 1854.

Ford, onetime governor of Illinois, gives some excellent accounts of the French settlers and the picturesque decay of their culture and colonies. Otherwise this is a most inferior work.

DE GANNES. *Memoir of De Gannes Concerning the Illinois Country.* Illinois State Historical Library, *Collections,* vol. 23. Springfield, 1934.

The author, who has never been identified ("De Gannes" may be merely the name of the copyist of the manuscript), tells his experiences among the Illinois Indians. This is an invaluable account, having rather more importance than many of the celebrated missionary relations.

HENNEPIN, LOUIS (Shea, John G. ed.). *A New Discovery of a Vast Country in America.* Chicago, 1903.

Father Hennepin, one of the most enigmatic characters of the history of American exploration, accompanied La Salle to the Illinois country, though the two men were out of sympathy with each other's aims and to some extent in their attitude to the aborigines. Unreliable as some of Hennepin's works are, this particular narrative is conceded a high place by historians, and forms one of the most fascinating accounts in all its field.

Hodge, Frederick Webb. *Handbook of American Indians.* Bureau of Ethnology, Smithsonian Institution, *Bulletin* 30. Washington, 1907.

A cyclopedia of the Amerinds. See articles on Algonkian, Illinois, Miami, Potawatomi.

Hunter, John D. *Memoirs of a Captivity Among the Indians from Childhood,* etc. . . . London, 1823.

Imlay, Gilbert. *Topographic Description of the Western Territory,* etc. . . . London, 1792.

The third London edition contains reprints of Thomas Hutchins' valuable *Topographical Description.*

Kenton, Edna (ed.). *The Indians of North America.* 2 vols. New York, 1927.

This is nothing less than a selection of the famous *Jesuit Relations,* the reports of the Jesuit missionaries to their bishops or other priestly superiors that forms one of the most precious documents in the history of the New World. Fortunately, Miss Kenton's book stresses the Illinois missions. The footnotes, by specialists in the subject, elucidate and deepen the value of the text.

KINZIE, JULIETTE A. *Waubun: The "Early Day" in the Northwest.* Chicago, 1901.

Mrs. Kinzie's famous book, originally printed in New York in 1856, throws light on the character of various Indian tribes of Illinois.

LAWSON, PUBLIUS V. *The Potawatomi.* In *The Wisconsin Archaeologist,* vol. 19, no. 2. 1920.

LONG, JOHN. *Voyages and Travels in the Years 1768-1788.* Chicago, 1922.

Trader and adventurer, John Long gave his candid impressions of Indians in the Chicago region. They are unflattering, but in agreement with the general impression which Americans had of the decadent period of Indian life.

MACLEOD, WILLIAM CHRISTIE. *The American Indian Frontier.* New York, 1928.

Some very suggestive and little-known facts about the structure of Indian society and its penetration by European life are here brought forward. The present writer merely finds himself in agreement, however, with those who are Macleod's equals in his science, in his impression that much that is entirely too sweeping in its assertions crops up in this book.

PARKMAN, FRANCIS. *La Salle and the Discovery of the Great West.* Boston, 1922.

See under Cox for another account of La Salle.

A Prairie Grove

SCHOOLCRAFT, HENRY. *Travels,* etc. . . . In Quaife, Milo Milton (ed.). *Pictures of Illinois One Hundred Years Ago.* Chicago, 1918.

Schoolcraft, an Indian ethnographer (according to his lights and times) and Indian linguist and sympathizer, gives a stirring account of Illinois scenery and a meeting with Indians at Chicago to arrange a treaty. He was one of the interpreters at this meeting and his specimens of Indian oratory are especially reliable. It will be remembered that Longfellow derived much of the material for *Hiawatha* from others of Schoolcraft's works.

SHEA, JOHN GILMARY (ed.). *Discovery and Exploration of the Mississippi Valley, with the Original Narratives of Marquette, Allouez, Membre, Hennepin, and Anastase Douay.* New York, 1852.

Shea was a brilliant and reliable editor. This book may suffice for the relation of Father Marquette, the first, as well as the best-loved, of all the missionaries to the Illinois country. His ability to combine simple Christian faith with a comprehension of the Indian character, and his death in the wilderness make of him a character of immortal nobility.

SKINNER, ALANSON BUCK. *The Mascoutens or Prairie Potawatomi.* In Public Museum of the City of Milwaukee, *Bulletin,* vol. 6. 1930.

This valuable study of the modern Mascoutens, comprising notes on their social life and ceremonies and their material culture, throws light upon the vanished Illinois tribes, for the Prairie Potawatomi were

A Prairie Grove

far more similar to the Illinois than to the Forest Potawatomi.

SMITH, HURON H. *Ethnobotany of the Meskwaki Indians.* In Public Museum of the City of Milwaukee, *Bulletin,* vol. 4, no. 2. 1928.

Although the Meskwaki tribe is merely related to the Illinois Indians, the flora of their territory is so nearly identical as to throw valuable light upon the practical and magical uses of plants in this region.

SPENCER, J. W. *Reminiscences of Pioneer Life,* etc. . . . Davenport, 1872.

This is a good sample of the "old Indian fighter" attitude toward the aborigines.

STRONG, WILLIAM DUNCAN. *Indian Tribes of the Chicago Region.* Field Museum Anthropology *Leaflet,* no. 24. Chicago, 1926.

TANNER, JOHN (James, Edwin, ed.). *Narrative of Captivity and Adventures of John Tanner . . . Among the Indians of the Interior,* etc. . . . New York, 1830.

A short edition for junior readers under the title of *Gray Hawk* edited by James Macaulay appeared in London in 1897. This was the only edition available to the present writer.

TONTY, HENRI DE. *Relation of Henry de Tonty Concerning the Explorations of La Salle from 1678 to 1683.* Chicago, 1898.

Tonty (often spelled Tonti) was La Salle's gallant lieutenant, and his account of holding the Illinois forts for his absent and fated leader is among the most moving narrations of the North American wilderness.

WISSLER, CLARK. *The American Indian.* New York, 1927.

A classic general cyclopedia of the Amerind.

PIONEER LIFE, IMMIGRATION, AND SETTLEMENT; PRAIRIES AND GROVES AS ENVIRONMENT

ALVORD, CLARENCE W. *Trade and Land Speculation.* Illinois State Historical Library, *Collections,* vol. 11. Springfield, 1918.

BEACH, RICHARD. *A Letter from Illinois Written in 1836.* In Illinois State Historical Society, *Journal,* vol. 3, no. 3. 1910.

Gives prices of commodities.

BOGGESS, ARTHUR C. *The Settlement of Illinois, 1778-1830.* In Chicago Historical Society, *Collections,* vol. 5. 1908.

BRUNSON, ALFRED. *A Methodist Circuit Rider's Horseback Tour from Pennsylvania to Wisconsin.* In *Wisconsin Historical Collections,* vol. 15. 1900.

Consists largely in notes on men and scenes in northern Illinois in the year 1835.

BUCK, SOLON JUSTUS. *Illinois in 1818.* In *Centennial History of Illinois,* introductory volume, 2nd edition. Chicago, 1918.

The chapters on "The Indians and the Fur Trade,"

A Prairie Grove

"The Public Lands," "The Extent of Settlement," "The Pioneers," and "Social Conditions" have proved especially valuable.

BURLEND, REBECCA. *A True Picture of Emigration, or Fourteen Years in the Interior of North America.* Chicago, 1936.

This originally appeared anonymously in London in 1841, and is a deeply moving story of English immigrants' life as prairie pioneers.

CARTWRIGHT, PETER. *Autobiography.* Cincinnati, 1856.

The life of a forthright Methodist circuit rider in Illinois from 1825-53, of value only as exhibiting the mentality of the author's profession in that age.

FARNHAM, ELIZA W. *Life in Prairie Land.* New York, 1846.

This seems to the present writer the most vivid account of prairie pioneering in Illinois which he has discovered. The author, a New England woman, unconsciously exhibits her own mental growth during her prairie experiences, changing over gradually from a certain sense of congenital superiority to the attitude of the first-generation Western pioneer of the most admirable type. Some of her chapters are undoubtedly fanciful, that is to say fictional reconstructions of typical events and scenes, but the author has fairly well indicated all changes from reminiscence to imagination and back again.

GILLMORE, PARKER (pseud. "Ubique"). *Prairie Farms and Prairie Folk.*

A Prairie Grove

KINZIE, JULIETTE A. *Waubun: The "Early Day" in the Northwest.* New York, 1856.

This same work, discussed under the first section of this bibliography, is notable for its beautiful descriptions of prairie and grove scenery in the eighteen-twenties and eighteen-thirties.

MAJOR, NOAH H. *The Pioneers of Morgan County.* In Indiana Historical Society, *Publications,* vol. 5, no. 5. 1915.

This is a most picturesque and valuable account of the pioneers of the forest regions of the Middle West.

MORLEIGH. *Life in the West; Back-wood Leaves and Prairie Flowers: . . . Extracts from the Note Book of Morleigh in Search of an Estate.* London, 1842.

The author, not identified beyond the reference in the title, came to the Chicago region from England with the intention of farming. Like many other English immigrants he looked the prospects over disdainfully, returned at once to England, and wrote an unflattering account of Cousin Jonathan and his land. Nevertheless the account is vivid and in many ways probably quite true. In particular it is of interest as showing the great contrast between the scenery, game, flora, and human types of the eighteen-forties, and the rhapsodic accounts of visitors and settlers in the earlier decades.

PAXSON, FREDERICK L. *History of the American Frontier, 1763-1893.* New York, 1924.

A classic.

A Prairie Grove

PECK, JOHN M. *Forty Years of Pioneer Life.* Philadelphia, 1864.

    The point of view of a Baptist missionary.

POOLEY, WILLIAM VIPOND. *Settlement of Illinois from 1830-1850.* In University of Wisconsin, *Bulletin,* no. 22. (*History series,* vol. 1, no. 4.)

    A closely reasoned and analytic account, illustrating clearly the contrast between the settlers of southern Illinois and those of the northern part of the state, the former mostly Southerners and a forest people, the latter Northerners who arrived at the beginning of the industrial revolution and armed with its technique. The importance of the island groves, and the peculiar conditions of prairie life as settlers first experienced them, are clearly set forth.

REYNOLDS, JOHN. *Pioneer History of Illinois.* Chicago, 1897.

    The author has written a fairly vivid account, based upon much firsthand knowledge of pioneer life, but it is without the mental equipment of an historian.

TILLSON, CHRISTINA HOLMES. *A Woman's Story of Pioneer Illinois.* Chicago, 1919.

    Originally this work appeared in 1870 under the title *Reminiscences of Early Life in Illinois, 1819 to 1827.* Together with Mrs. Burlend's book and Mrs. Farnham's, it forms one of the three best accounts of a woman immigrant's experiences of prairie pioneering. Women have, in fact, done much better than the men in the way of vivid memoirs.

A Prairie Grove

THE FAUNA OF THE GROVES AND THE ILLINOIS PRAIRIE

(The following include only zoological works; game animals as seen from the point of view of pioneers and sportsmen are mentioned many times in the foregoing citations.)

ALLEN, J. A. *The American Bisons, Living and Extinct.* In Geological Survey of Kentucky, *Memoirs*, vol. 1. 1876. (Also in Museum of Comparative Zoology, Harvard College, *Memoirs*, vol. 4. 1876.)

This is the most compendious account of the buffalo or bison. More than once it contradicts popular conceptions, and even accounts of early travelers and others, about the life of the bison and the formation of the herd.

BENT, ARTHUR C. *Life Histories of North American Gallinaceous Birds.* In U. S. National Museum, *Bulletin*, no. 162. Smithsonian Institution, Washington, 1932.

This volume deals with passenger pigeons, prairie chickens, and wild turkeys. Bent's monumental and still unfinished series is cited here, rather than his distinguished sources which include Audubon, Alexander Wilson, and other ornithological authorities, because he has extracted the best of them all and brought them together in one place.

—— *Life Histories of North American Gulls and Terns.* In U. S. National Museum, *Bulletin*, no. 113. Smithsonian Institution, Washington, 1921.

A Prairie Grove

―――― *Life Histories of North American Marsh Birds.* In U. S. National Museum, *Bulletin,* no. 35. Smithsonian Institution, Washington, 1926.

This volume deals with rails, cranes, and herons.

―――― *Life Histories of North American Shore Birds, Order Limicolae* (part 1). In U. S. National Museum, *Bulletin,* no. 142. Smithsonian Institution, Washington, 1927.

―――― *Life Histories of North American Shore Birds, Order Limicolae* (part 2). In U. S. National Museum, *Bulletin,* no. 146. Smithsonian Institution, Washington, 1929.

CATON, JOHN DEAN. *The Antelope and Deer of America.* Boston, 1877.

Much the most thoroughgoing study of the native *Cervidae.* Caton raised practically every species in his park in northern Illinois.

CORY, CHARLES B. *The Mammals of Illinois and Wisconsin.* In Field Museum of Natural History, *Publication,* no. 153. (*Zoology series,* vol. 11.) Chicago, 1912.

KENNICOTT, ROBERT. *The Quadrupeds of Illinois Injurious and Beneficial to the Farmer.* In U. S. Patent Office, *Report of Agriculture* for 1857. Washington, 1858.

Kennicott, one of the foremost Middle Western naturalists, and the first important native naturalist, writes of the mammals of the island groves and prairies out of firsthand knowledge.

A Prairie Grove

Lyon, Marcus Ward, Jr. *The Mammals of Indiana.* Notre Dame, Indiana, 1936.

This excellent work includes a great many citations from old accounts of quadruped life and hunting in pioneer times.

Mershon, W. B. *The Passenger Pigeon.* New York, 1907.

Extracts from practically all the best old accounts of the pigeons have here been brought together.

Seton, Ernest Thompson. *Lives of Game Animals.* 4 vols. New York City, 1929.

This comprehensive work selects citations from all the leading life histories of North American quadrupeds, such as those of Audubon and Bachman.

Thacker, Henry. *Muskrat Hunting.* Wallingford, Conn., 1867.

Among other things, this rare little work discusses the animal life and scenery along the Desplaines River, and the waterways and portages of the Chicago region.

Woodruff, Frank M. *The Birds of the Chicago Area.* In Chicago Academy of Sciences, Natural History Survey, *Bulletin,* no. 6. 1907.

In this catalogue are brought together a great many notes on the now rare extinct bird life from publications and records of decades with a richer avifauna.

A Prairie Grove

FLORA OF THE ILLINOIS PRAIRIES, OAK OPENINGS, AND ISLAND GROVES

GLEASON, A. H. *An Isolated Prairie Grove and Its Phytogeographical Significance.* In *Botanical Gazette*, vol. 53. 1912.

—— *The Vegetational History of the Middle West.* In Association of American Geographers, *Annals*, vol. 12. 1923.

MOSHER, EDNA. *The Grasses of Illinois.* In University of Illinois Agricultural Experiment Station, *Bulletin*, no. 205. 1918.

SAMPSON, H. C. *An Ecological Survey of the Prairie Vegetation of Illinois.* In Illinois State Laboratory of Natural History, *Bulletin*, no. 13. 1921.

VESTAL, ARTHUR G. *A Black-soil Prairie Station in Northeastern Illinois.* In Torrey Botanical Club, *Bulletin*, vol. 41. 1914.

WEAVER, J. E. and THIEL, A. F. *Ecological Studies in the Tension Zone between Prairie and Woodland.* In University of Nebraska *Botanical Survey* (new series), vol. 1. 1917.

WEAVER, J. E. and FITZPATRICK, T. J. *The Prairie.* In *Ecological Monographs*, vol. 4, no. 2. 1934.

WOODWARD, JOHN. *Origin of the Prairies in Illinois.* In *Botanical Gazette*, vol. 77. 1924.

A NOTE ABOUT THE AUTHOR

DONALD CULROSS PEATTIE *was born in 1898 in Chicago. In 1922 he was graduated* cum laude *from Harvard, and thereupon entered the Office of Foreign Seed and Plant Introduction in the Department of Agriculture at Washington, where he spent three years in botanical research. He then became a free-lance, publishing novels and nonfiction, as well as such technical works as the* Flora of the Indiana Dunes. *After six years abroad, he returned to America and the interpretation of its Nature.* An Almanac for Moderns *was published in 1935 and was awarded the first annual Gold Medal of the Limited Editions Club, as the book written by an American author during the previous three years most likely to become a classic. It was followed by* Singing in the Wilderness, A Salute to John James Audubon. *The next year he wrote* Green Laurels: The Lives and Achievements of the Great Naturalists, *and in the spring of 1937 his* A Book of Hours *appeared. Donald Peattie is married to Louise Redfield Peattie, herself a writer, with whom he has collaborated on several books. They have three sons.*